In Hospital and Camp

In Hospital and Camp

The Civil War through the Eyes of Its Doctors and Nurses

Compiled by

Harold Elk Straubing

STACKPOLE
BOOKS

Copyright © 1993 by Harold Elk Straubing

Published by
STACKPOLE BOOKS
Cameron and Kelker Streets
P.O. Box 1831
Harrisburg, PA 17105

Printed in the United States of America

First edition

10 9 8 7 6 5 4 3 2 1

Library of Congress Cataloging-in-Publication Data

Straubing, Harold Elk, 1918–
    In hospital and camp : the Civil War through the eyes of its
doctors and nurses / Harold Elk Straubing. — 1st ed.
        p.   cm.
    Includes bibliographical references and index.
    ISBN 0-8117-1631-7
    1. United States—History—Civil War, 1861–1865—Medical care.
    2. Medicine, Military—United States—History—19th century.
    I. Title.
    E621.S86   1993
    973.7'75—dc20   92-25328
                                                              CIP

This book is humbly dedicated to the medical profession and especially to Doctors Sant P. Chawla, Jeffrey J. Eckardt, Malcolm Alan Lesavoy, Gerald Rosen, and Ronald W. Thompson, whose talents and efforts gave me another chance at life.

No more shall the war-cry sever,
  Or the widening rivers be red;
Our anger is banished forever
    When are laureled the graves of our dead!
    Under the sod and the dew,
      Waiting the judgment day;—
  Love and tears, for the Blue;
    Tears and love, for the Gray.
                                    —*F. M. Finch*

Contents

Introduction

THE VAST LITERARY output dealing with the experience of individuals in the American Civil War covers almost every aspect of life and death during that frenzied and troubled period. Books were, and still are, published on generals and admirals who dealt with the war as a huge chess game on land and sea, moving men up and down the fighting lines. They were followed by supplies as the wounded were moved toward the rear, the dead buried where they fell.

The range of the war was massive, and most writing impersonal. The stories of large concentrations of men and their battles were told in bold brush strokes. Other writings were diaries and reminiscences of individuals who relived their experiences on paper to let their children and grandchildren know of the terrible price each had to pay in trying either to hold this nation together or to split it asunder. These tales were generally very narrow in scope, encompassing the actions and reactions of individuals in their immediate vicinity.

One branch of the service that seldom recorded its battle history was the medical corps. Doctors and nurses had an overview of an entire sector. They dealt with the soldiers, the wounded, the diseased, and the dying. They were never too far behind the fighting front lines, often in the battle itself as forces crisscrossed the same land. On occasion they found themselves in enemy territory and then, of necessity, put aside their medical kits and took up weapons.

The doctors filled medical journals and technical tomes about their new operating techniques and other discoveries, but very few of them recorded their on-the-scene experiences. It is in this manner that they enriched American medical annals. Previously American medical texts lacked imagination, being based chiefly on Great Britain's medical writings, a practice that prompted Dr.

Oliver Holmes to complain that the American surgical press was simply "putting British portraits in American frames."[1]

To understand the status of the medical corps of the Union Army in 1861 fully is to realize that the country entered the war totally unprepared. Merit had less to do with promotion in the prewar army than with seniority. The Medical Department chief, War of 1812 veteran Thomas Lawson, was over 80 years of age and dying of cancer.[2] Morale was poor under this recognized martinet. Men sometimes went up to ten years at frontier posts before he would grant them a 60-day furlough. He continually pared the department, cutting its budget and making available only the barest of supplies. There was a minimum inventory of medicine, bandages, and medical tools.[3]

Because of these conditions, many were unwilling to remain in the U.S. Medical Corps. At the war's start a quarter of the surgeons and assistant surgeons resigned either to go with the Confederates or into private practice. The Union Army was left with 98 medical officers.[4]

At the war's beginning, hygienic conditions in the camp that housed the volunteer army were deplorable. Regular army troops, accustomed to discipline, managed to keep their quarters clean according to military rules whereas volunteers were very lax. As a result disease was rampant wherever they bivouacked. The Union troops stationed about Washington D.C. were so racked with illness that a public outcry resulted in the formation of a Sanitary Commission to look after the needs and interests of the volunteer army.

The need for medical men was acute, but the call up to fill the vacancies was slow. Initial appointees came from among yet-uncommissioned applicants who had already passed their competency testing. With General Lawson leaving his position in the medical corps, 116 new candidates volunteered, and 62 received appointments.[5]

[1] H.H. Cunningham, *Doctors In Gray* (Baton Rouge, La., 1958), 17.
[2] Stewart Brooks, *Civil War Medicine* (Springfield, Ill., 1966), 12.
[3] George W. Adams, *Doctors in Blue* (New York, 1952), 4.
[4] *Ibid.*, 4.
[5] Adams, *Doctors in Blue,* 9.

Chaos compounded confusion. The methods of appointment to the Medical Corps differed from state to state. There was a wide variance in the technical skills and competence offered by these newly inducted doctors.[6]

The editor of a leading medical journal complained in late June 1861: "We may estimate by hundreds the number of unqualified persons who have received the endorsement of these bodies [medical examining boards] as capable surgeons and assistant surgeons of regiments. Indeed, these examinations in some cases have been so conducted as to prove the merest farce. . . . Whoever has examined the list of surgeons passed by the different State examining committees must have regretted to find so few names of eminent surgeons."[7]

While many doctors were not certified to hold their positions, others became alcoholics and in drunken stupors left wards unattended, and still others were accused of refreshing their anatomy studies by performing surgery upon patients who were anesthetized awaiting amputations.

The amazing statistics reveal that of the 360,222 Union soldiers who lost their lives, 110,100 were victims of Confederate attacks, 26,872 died in accidents and causes other than illness, and the balance of 224,580 perished because of various diseases. There were more than 470,000 cases of wounds and injuries North and South, and almost 600,000 cases of sicknesses, notably pneumonia, tuberculosis, scurvy, and rheumatism, with typhoid, scarlet fever, and yellow fever trailing. Both armies suffered equally with disease. An epidemic of childhood diseases, from chicken pox to measles, would break out in the Union and Confederate forces whenever new recruits were housed together.

While the records of Confederate Army casualties are somewhat sketchy, they are equally outrageous: 94,000 men were killed in battle, and 164,000 died of disease.[8]

Smallpox vaccination was known long before 1861, but the failure to make immunization a standard part of induction procedure was overlooked, and that oversight led to many needless cases of

---

[6] Adams, *Doctors in Blue,* 10.

[7] *Ibid.,* 10. Quoting the New York *Tribune.*

[8] E. B. Long, *The Civil War Day by Day* (New York, 1971), 710–11.

this disease. There was a general disregard of army regulations concerning physical examinations because of the different roles states played in mobilization.

In one instance officers conducted physical examinations for new inductees by having them march past the medical director. Those who limped or failed to stand straight as they marched were rejected; all others passed into the army. This was contrary to the regulation that required each recruit to have a physical examination while stripped to the skin. Because of this laxity, not only were many ill men inducted in the army, but also young women disguised as boys became soldiers. In many cases they carried on this charade until they were wounded and needed medical care.[9]

Drafted epileptic, tubercular, syphilitic, and hernia cases were soon in hospitals taking up space, denying beds to the wounded. Many of the diseased recruits contaminated camps where little or nothing was known about sanitation or the role of insects such as lice, mosquitoes, and flies in spreading diarrhea and malaria. Typhoid was spread by contaminated water supplies.

Latrines, or "sinks," were standard Civil War fixtures. These were often shallow trenches left uncovered and located so near to living quarters that the soldiers were subjected to a nauseating, malodorous stench. Some men, either too modest to use the public sinks or too sensitive to the odor, improvised private toilets in the camp area. The men would void urine anywhere they desired, especially at night, adding to the camp's fetid scent.

There was no provision for sterilizing water; purification kits were unknown. Troops filled their canteens in the Mississippi River. In some instances medical authorities would recommend boiling or filtering water before drinking, but this advice was generally ignored. Thousands of men suffering with violent diarrhea found their way into hospitals.

Garbage disposal was negligent and sloppy. Camp streets and spaces between the tents were usually littered with refuse, decomposed food, and rubbish of all description. The waste of butchered animals was tossed into pits near the camp along with horse manure.

---

[9] Adams, *Doctors in Blue,* 12.

Cleanliness was neglected despite army regulations that required a daily washing of hands and face, the washing of feet at least twice a month, and a complete bath once or twice a month. Because of cold weather and a lack of facilities and opportunity, men often went months without bathing or washing their clothes.[10]

Another cause for sickness was the poor diet afforded the troops. The food staple was salt pork and beans. Everything was fried in a sea of boiling bacon grease. Rice, beans, and flour mixed with water shaped into small cakes joined in the bubbling grease. When meat was available, that too was tossed into the cauldron. A medical officer who attempted to save his men from what he called "death by the frying pan" suggested to the soldiers that they spear the meat with a stick and hold it over the fire. His advice was disregarded. A military surgeon declared that "beans killed more than bullets."[11]

There was a widespread lack of fresh vegetables and fruit that helped to swell the sick list. It also slowed the recovery of the ill and the wounded and was responsible for an increase in the mortality rate.

Communicable diseases played no favorites. They worked both sides of the battlefield. They were a factor in the failure of the Confederate Army of the Northwest's Cheat Mountain campaign in September 1861. Gen. Robert E. Lee had about 11,000 men in his six brigades; more than Union Gen. Joseph J. Reynolds' opposing force. Some of Lee's regiments were composed of very new recruits, none more than a few months in the army. Almost half the soldiers became ill at the same time. These men required nursing care and were not available for combat. They consumed needed food, delayed incoming supplies as the sick were moved to the rear, clogging roads with commandeered vehicles, and had to be attended to by other military personnel, thereby further depleting the fighting ranks. The major diseases that played havoc with the Confederates also plagued the Union forces: measles, dysentery, diarrhea, pneumonia, typhoid fever, malaria, diphtheria, and rheumatism.[12]

---

[10] Adams, *Doctors in Blue*, 15–17.
[11] Adams, *Doctors in Blue*, 16.
[12] Paul Steiner, *Disease in the Civil War* (Springfield, Ill.,1968), 53–54.

When General Lee learned how sick his army was, he wrote to his wife, "We have a great deal of sickness among the soldiers, and now those on the sick list would form an army. The measles is still among them, though I hope it is dying out. But it is a disease which though light in childhood is severe in manhood and prepares the system for other attacks. The constant rain, with no shelter but tents, have aggravated it. All these drawbacks, with impassible roads, have paralyzed our efforts."[13]

In the antebellum era the need for physicians was great throughout the country. In some sections of the South, people were prone to special diseases, requiring doctors with specific knowledge in these areas. There were several prestigious medical schools in the South, but the demand for doctors was so strong that new "medical" schools, unregulated by any requirements or laws, were organized. Anyone with money could receive a diploma and the privilege of practicing medicine. Schools with outlandish theories and ideas pertaining to medical practice flourished. There were those that specialized in electrochemical baths and others that believed in the curative powers of electric shock therapy. There were some who practiced medicine as mesmerists, herbalists, clairvoyants, spiritualists with healing powers, chromothermalists, and Native American doctors. By 1850 it was said that everyone was allowed to practice medicine—and just about everyone did.

The closed minds of many of the legitimate medical practitioners took no note of the latest scientific discoveries, and therefore many new advances were disregarded or overlooked. One glaring instance is the use of the clinical thermometer. Although it was introduced almost two hundred years before the Civil War, there is evidence that fewer than six thermometers were used by the Union Army during the conflict.

As a general rule, the recognized medical schools in the South were on a par with those of the North. All schools were showing some interest in a new French medical theory related to pathology, which claimed that there were diseases that could be traced to lesions in various bodily organs, and therefore those organs should be excised to effect a cure. American doctors began to turn to the

---

[13] Steiner, *Disease in the Civil War*, 53–54.

lancet and the scalpel, especially in frontier towns, where the inhabitants, for some reason, were willing to expose themselves to additional surgical risk.

Most operative surgery by Southern medical officers was performed upon patients with chloroform as the anesthetic. The medical director of the Confederate Medical Corps, Hunter McGuire, claimed that chloroform was administered more than twenty-eight thousand times in his corps, and no death was ever attributed to its use.

Surgical achievements of Confederate surgeons brought praise from the medical profession. Because of a lack of surgical instruments, they improvised with materials at hand, as in one case when a surgeon amputated a man's hand with a carpenter's saw. In another case, a surgeon confronted with a sudden secondary hemorrhage successfully ligated the external carotid artery with the assistance of a pair of retractors improvised from the iron bail of a water bucket. According to one surgeon: "The pliant bark of a tree made for him a good tourniquet; the juice of the green persimmon, a styptic; a knitting needle, with its point sharply bent, a tenaculum, and a pen-knife in his hand, a scalpel." A table fork with all tines removed but one, which was bent, was used to elevate the bone in a depressed skull fracture.[14]

Doctors of both sides on the battlefield had to meet the challenge of wounds caused by the rifle's minié ball. (In official records the bullet was referred to as the "conoidal ball.") For both sides, the minié ball was responsible about 94 percent of the time for casualties, and shell and canister about 6 percent of the time. The saber and the bayonet were the least effective and the least used, accounting for less than four of every one thousand wounds.[15]

There were very few doctors who had treated gunshot wounds before the war. The field was entirely foreign to them. It is no wonder that when gunshots penetrated the abdomen and the head, the surgeons couldn't cope with the wounds, and about 90 percent were fatal. In the event the small intestine was involved, death was inevitable. There was a 60 percent mortality rate with minié balls that penetrated the chest. A minié ball striking an arm

---

[14] Cunningham, *Doctors in Gray*, 230–31.
[15] William C. Davis, *Fighting Men of The Civil War* (London, 1989), 47.

or a leg usually led to amputation. If infection did not set in, the patient could be saved.

The death rate from minié ball wounds was high because of the savage way the balls tore through the flesh. Just the look of such a wound was enough to frighten the average surgeon. Extensive bleeding followed by shock was common, and infection was assured as the ball tore through the flesh, dragging with it bits of uniform and dirt. The lead ball mushroomed as it continued its way through flesh and bone. Infection often led to gangrene, and the amputation of the outer limbs continued until death.[16]

Doctors were not immune to flying lead. In the Federal Forces, Medical Corps casualties showed that 42 were killed in battle, 83 were wounded, 290 died of disease or accidents, and 4 died in Confederate prisons. Confederate statistics are not readily available, for most records have disappeared over the years.

The men and women who entered the medical service during the Civil War were faced with an almost insurmountable challenge. They offered comfort to wounded or diseased men. Some of their experiences are recounted here, recalling the hardships and the frustrations they encountered in their efforts to serve. In a war, all at the battlefront live through their own personal terror. In this book, several doctors and nurses who served during these terrible, perilous years tell where and how they endured their own hell.

The value of turning to these individuals' letters and personal memoirs is the insight we gain into the writers themselves. Some strike the professional pose; others reveal the crybaby or mama's boy. The drama in which they find themselves reveals their character and their soul. We see the war through their eyes.

The valor and bravery of the armed forces on both sides of the fighting line have been, and continue to be, an inspiration to all Americans.

---

[16] Cunningham, *Doctors in Gray*, 220.

Letters from a Surgeon of the Civil War

by John G. Perry, as compiled by Martha Derby Perry

JOHN G. PERRY entered Harvard College in 1858 with a few personal problems, the leading one being the length of schooling that faced him, including the time needed for Medical School—and that was only a matter of concern to him because he was in love.

In order to hasten his marriage date to Martha Derby, he decided to abandon his college life and attend the Scientific School, which offered shorter terms and collateral studies; then he would enter Medical School and later the hospital service. In the spring of 1862, the government issued a call for volunteer contract assistant surgeons to serve in the military hospitals in order to avoid detaching the commissioned assistant surgeons, who were needed on the battlefields. The medical student in general was best adapted to this service, and it well suited the needs of Perry, for he could use his experience toward his medical degree. He made application and was accepted. His orders requested that he report to Surgeon General Cuyler at Fortress Monroe and pick up his assignment at the Chesapeake Hospital. He received permission to fit himself for his final examinations at the Boston Medical School by means of experience in army hospitals rather than through the usual routines of study.

But in time of war nothing moves along as planned. John Perry was assigned to General Grant's forces before the Wilderness Campaign from May to June 1864.

After the Gettysburg Campaign, the Union Army of the Potomac under General Meade entered on no decisive moves until early in May 1864. Then the Northern commander in chief, General Grant, led Meade's army across the Rapidon River into the Wilderness, a wild and tangled forest, gloomy and foreboding, an abandoned mining area with few roads about ten miles west of Fredericksburg.

Grant planned to get through the Wilderness onto cleared land before trying to destroy the smaller Confederate Army of Northern Virginia under General Lee. But Lee advanced on the Federals while they were still in that tangled undergrowth, causing Grant to face about and order an attack. The terrain made the Battle of the Wilderness a disjointed and bloody fight. After the repulse of a Union attack on May 6, through the opportune arrival of the 1st Corps under General Longstreet,

11

Lee counterattacked, and the battle became stabilized as General Burnside and his forces joined Grant.

General Lee's right wing pushed the Union forces toward Spotsylvania Courthouse, about twelve miles to the southeast. In two days of fighting, the Union Army lost 17,500 men of its force of more than 100,000. The Confederate Army lost 8,000 of the more than 61,000 engaged in the battle.[1]

The fighting took on a nightmarish quality. Since the enemy wasn't seen, officers charged, leading their men with compass in hand or following gun flashes, often stumbling upon the enemy and prompting a chaotic melee of killing and maiming.

Lee anticipated Grant's next move and was soon entrenched, so that in the battle of Spotsylvania Courthouse (May 8–19, 1864), Grant unsuccessfully hammered away at the Confederate lines. The bloodiest fighting of this battle occurred May 12, when the Union assault on the salient forming the Confederate center was repulsed after initial success. Lee confronted Grant's next move from a position south of the North Anna River, so impregnable that Grant would not attack. The month of June found the armies near Richmond, where Grant made another unsuccessful frontal assault on his strongly entrenched enemy. In the battle of Cold Harbor (June 3, 1864), the Union lost 7,000 men in a few hours, the most horrible slaughter of the war.

After several days of trench fighting, Grant withdrew his forces, crossed the James River, and moved against Petersburg. Grant had lost about 60,000 men in the campaign, and although Lee's army sustained a proportionately larger loss of 20,000, it was hardly destroyed.[2]

John Perry served with Grant's forces through these bloody days, and his letters, collected by his wife, are an excellent record of a period racked with confusion and uncertainty.

---

[1] Bruce Catton, *The American Heritage Picture History of the Civil War*, Vol. II., (New York, 1960).
[2] Ibid.

May 3rd 1864

At last orders have come to move, and now commences the campaign of 1864 under Grant. How will it end? It has begun, at least in secrecy, for no one seems to know what is to be done beyond marching, and that marching under Grant means moving towards the enemy.

As is usual, after a winter's rest and idleness in camp, the men open a new campaign with an excess of spirit. We crossed the river without opposition, and late in the afternoon struck the Fredericksburg Turnpike, which we followed in what seemed to be a westerly direction. Before long we heard sharp musketry firing, toward which we made our way, and about dusk struck a road running south and at right angles to that which we were on. Here we halted, and were told to bivouac under arms against a rail fence, which stood between us and the thick woods where the firing was. The woods were so dense that we could not distinguish the artillery firing from the rest of the reports, but the sound continued until dark.

Hot firing opened at daybreak, and it seemed so near that when orders came to "fall in line," the new German recruits simply would not obey. They were so terrified that they lay like logs, and no amount of rough handling, even with bayonets, had any effect upon them whatever. The order to advance was given; still these fellows clung to the ground with faces buried in the grass, and, although some were shot by the officers, literally nothing moved them.

"Go on," was the next order, and on we went, leaving the miserable wretches lying there,—a few may have fallen into line, but I doubt it. We pushed forward, and very quickly were walking over rows of dead bodies piled at times two and three deep, and they lay in lines, exactly as if mowed down, showing the havoc of yesterday's fight. These lines seemed to be equally distant one from the other, as if each body of men advanced a certain distance, received a volley, then advanced again, and received another. I noticed a man near me in the ranks at this time singing a hymn with all his might and main. His head was thrown back, his mouth wide open, and he seemed completely absorbed in the emotion called forth to the hymn, which made him oblivious of all surroundings. I watched him curiously, and understood that it was an instinctive impulse on his part to try to hold his senses together and to steady himself under the well-nigh unendurable strain. As long as I saw the fellow, he kept his place without stumbling, and obeyed orders.

The right of the Twentieth bore on the turnpike for about two miles, when we met the enemy and the fighting began. I stationed myself just behind the regiment in the woods on the side of the road, and opened my hospital paraphernalia; then sent the stretcher-bearers over the field. Soon I was deep in work.

Meanwhile reserves were brought up, and among them I saw General Bartlett at the head of his brigade; but we had time only for a passing salute. Shortly after that an orderly came towards me, leading a horse, with an officer in the saddle, back from the front. The man was bent far over the horse's neck, bleeding profusely from a wound in the head, and white as death. To my dismay, I saw it was Frank Bartlett, and I called his name again and again, but did not succeed in rousing him. Passing my finger into the wound before taking him from the saddle, I found the ball had not penetrated the bone, but had simply severed an artery in the scalp; so, pressing the artery till the steward brought a ligature, I shouted, "No harm done, old boy; this is only a flesh wound; you will be all right when I tie the artery and take a stitch or two"; and this good news seemed to bring him back to consciousness. I then laid him on the ground, and, after my work was finished, gave him a good horn of whiskey and very soon he rallied completely.

"John," he said, "I thought I was done for. Well, old fellow, if I'm all right, here goes!" and before I could stop him he had sprung into the saddle, waved his hand to me, and was off to the front again as fast as his horse could carry him. Such is the mental power of the two little words "death" and "life."

About the middle of the afternoon General Hancock rode up and told me to stop work and send all my wounded to the rear, as our troops were to fall back. This was tough and hot work, but I gathered all I could find and fell back with the rest.

May—, 1864

Something happened to me in this retreat to the crossroads which Hayward says was a heat-stroke, for there was no exposure to the sun, as I was sheltered by the woods. I remember nothing from the time General Hancock ordered me back and the wounded were sent off, till I found myself lying under an apple-tree, with "Uncle Nathan" sponging my head with cold water. My steward says that while on the retreat I talked incoherently, then ran and shouted, until he guided me to the Division Hospital where I fell unconscious.

When I came to my senses sufficiently to sit up, Hayward told me that our little Abbott (at that time major, but acting colonel) had been shot through the abdomen and was dying. Dying! It was too dreadful to bear! Harry Abbott was an ideal man; an ideal officer, reverenced by his friends and deeply respected by all who know him. What will become of the Twentieth without him I cannot imagine; for he was its life, its discipline, and its success.[3]

The Wilderness, May 7th, 1864

I am safe and well, but our losses have been fearful. Poor Abbott is dead; Macy has a slight wound in the leg, but not dangerous; Bond is shot in the jaw, but doing well, Wallcott in the shoulder, and three others badly wounded.

During the first day's fight I was with the regiment, but

---

[3] Major Abbott was shot through the body and lived for about eight hours after. He left all his money to the widows and orphans of the regiment. General Gibbon wrote to Abbott's father that Abbott was considered the most valuable officer in the corps.

now I am detailed to the hospital with Dr. Hayward, three
miles in the rear. I have been operating all day, and really
learned more in the way of experience than in all the time
since joining the regiment.

May 8th, 1864

Exhaustion and confusion worse confounded. Although perfectly well, I am tired and hot, having slept only a couple of
hours out of the last forty. We are still in the Wilderness, fighting our way inch by inch. The Twentieth has been in no
important action since I last wrote; our loss was then so terrible that they have spared us a little. Curtis is now in command, as Captain Paton was shot in the hand, but we cannot
induce him to go to the rear.

The Confederates fight determinedly, and their force facing
us is almost equal to ours, but we drive them each day. We are
both on a race for Richmond, and I wonder which will get the
inside track. If we do, our journey will be forty miles shorter
than theirs. Feeling as I do now, the thought of a forty-mile
march is quite repulsive. Grant seems determined to keep on
fighting, and either win or lose.

I now sit on the ground in the woods, leaning against a log
and writing on my knee. I am surrounded by soldiers, bon-
fires, and kicking horses,—but out of their reach, I assure you;
dust is sweeping over me like smoke; my face is black with
dirt and perspiration, clothes soiled and torn almost to pieces.
I am too tired to sleep, too tired to stand, and should dislike
to have you see me just now. Although we have been steadily
banging away at each other for a week, neither side has
gained much advantage. The enemy has gradually fallen
back, but each day shows a bold front.

The sun is just setting, thank God! but it is uncertain whether
we shall march all night, go out on picket, or lie down and
sleep,—the thought of sleep makes me absolutely silly. We never
know what we may be doing the next five minutes.

Hell! Here come two hundred "Johnnies" as prisoners. They
look defiant. I would in their place.

May 11th, 1864

My last writing was interrupted by orders to march, and fighting has been constant during the last three days. I am well, and incessantly at work over the wounded. I send this through a "Christian Commission" man, who goes North to-day.

May 13th, 1864

Fighting still,—ten days of it without intermission. I am so exhausted and nervous it is difficult to express myself; am operating day and night. This thing cannot last much longer, for one side or the other must yield from sheer exhaustion.

I am trying to gather together the Twentieth, but so far can find but two officers, no men, no colors. The only privates I have discovered are here in the hospital, and apparently there is almost nothing left of the dear old regiment.

Wilderness near Spottsylvania Court-house
Division Hospital
May 17th, 1864

Seventeen days since I have heard a word from the North. Not a single mail has been sent us since we left winter quarters.

We now find that six officers of the Twentieth are living (excluding Surgeon Hayward and myself) out of twenty who started with us. I am at present detailed to run the Division Hospital with Dr. Divenell.

Surgeons captured by the enemy are well treated and immediately paroled; in fact, they are scarcely noticed, much less disturbed. If one happens to have on a good pair of boots, he is generally relieved of them, which, under the circumstances, seems quite fair and proper. I have talked to many Confederates, and some of them admit terrible losses on their side, and seem discouraged. They tell me that we never fought so determinedly, so fiercely, or so long at a time as in this campaign, and that they could not possibly stand another

such siege. For ten days the battle raged each day, we being
the assaulting party. We have been comparatively quiet the
last two days, burying our dead.

Banks of the Mattapony River
May 22nd, 1864

It has rained every day for a week; the mud is several feet
deep, and the men thoroughly waterlogged, but nevertheless,
they are cheerful and ready to begin the contest again. I dread
the results of a fight, but must confess, as it seems the only
way of forcing the end, I want to go ahead.

We are not allowed mail facilities in this campaign, and our
only opportunities for sending letters North are by the wounded
on their way to the rear. I have material enough for fifty letters,
but dare not risk it in the hands of wounded privates.

Our corps, the Second, is separated from the main army. We
made a forced march to this place, which is called Milford,
night before last and yesterday. We are two miles from Bowling
Green, by the Fredericksburg and Richmond Railroad, and on
the banks of the Mattapony River. General Hancock made this
move successfully, but with a loss of about fifty of his cavalry.
This is the route by which General Lee sent all his wounded to
Richmond. We are almost directly in General Lee's rear,—at
any rate, so far in his rear that it is probable he will have to fall
back in order to fight us. We have entrenched ourselves as
securely as we can, and the river covers both our flanks. The
Second corps is estimated at twenty-five thousand men.

On one of the recent days of fighting, at early dawn the
troops were in line, when the order was given to charge without noise. While on the run,—I following with my hospital
steward about twenty yards in the rear of the men,—we saw
in a clump of bushes a pair of boots with the soles up, as if the
owner had taken a headlong leap into the hedge. Stopping to
investigate, I pulled out Captain Kelliher of the Twentieth. He
was horribly mangled about the face and neck, as if from

a shell or solid shot; yet no gun had been heard, and no one seen to leave the ranks.

I found him bleeding freely from a laceration of the subclavian artery, showing that the injury could only have been received a moment before, else he would have bled to death. He was still living, though unconscious, and after tying the artery, so as to stop the hemorrhage, he was placed on a stretcher and carried to the rear. The fighting lasted but a short time; as the Confederates were but partially surprised, they rallied and held us in check.

As soon as the Division Hospital tents were up, I had Kelliher taken to Dr. Hayward, who, finding him still alive, though yet unconscious, decided to remove the shattered bones and to clean and stitch the wounds, so as to give him all the comfort possible, but with no hope of saving his life. Under the chloroform the captain rallied still more, and a few hours after our work was finished he finally became conscious. Dr. Hayward had removed the shattered lower jaw, the whole arm, including a shoulder-blade, or scapula, the clavicle or collarbone, and a large part of the first two ribs on the same side of the body, as all these broken bones were lacerating the flesh, and the surfaces of the lung were exposed. When the operation was completed, the line of suture for closing the wounds ran from the ear to within an inch or two of the pelvis.

I placed the patient under my shelter tent, and ordered the steward to feed and stimulate him as directed. In the night it rained so hard that I dug a trench about him to keep him from being drenched and chilled. The following day we were ordered to push on, and to place the wounded, who were unable to march, in army wagons destined for the "White House Landing," which was twenty miles away. What was to become of poor Kelliher? Surely he could never survive such a strain, even though at the time he was doing well. After much deliberation I decided to consult the captain himself, and to follow his decision. In presenting to him the situation, I offered to remain with him in case he wished to be left, and told him that we must simply make up our minds to be cap-

tured by the enemy; but his answer was clear and prompt: "I
will go to the White House Landing, Doctor, and, Doctor, I
shall live." So, doing what was possible to make him comfortable with the use of straw and grass by way of a mattress,
I bade him good-bye, never dreaming that he could survive
such a journey.[4]

Two Miles from Hanover Junction
May 24th, 1864

I can scratch only a few lines, being up to my elbows in blood.
Oh, the fatigue and endless work we surgeons have! About
one night in three to sleep in, and then we are so nervous and
played out that sleep is impossible.

The hospital is fast filling up with poor fellows who last
night charged upon the enemy's works on the other side of
the river. We are some fifteen miles nearer Richmond than
when I last wrote, and the strongest works of the Confederacy
are at this point and at the South Anna River. They were
thrown up during the first year of the war.

It looks now as if we should still compel the enemy to fall
back. We have had a deal of forced marching lately, and the
heat has been almost intolerable. At times it has seemed as if
the sun's rays would lay us out, yet we march all day, and
through volumes upon volumes of dense dust. News has just
come that the Confederates are falling back, and so I suppose
we must pack our wounded into wagons and move after
them with all the speed possible.

It seems to me I am quite callous to death now, and that I
could see my dearest friend die without much feeling. This
condition tells a long story which, under other circumstances,
could scarcely be imagined. During the last three weeks I have

---

[4] (Original author's note) Captain Kelliher, after complete recovery, rejoined the
Twentieth and was commissioned its major, and remained in active service with the
regiment till the end of the war.

seen probably no less than two thousand deaths, and among them those of many dear friends. I have witnessed hundreds of men shot dead, have walked and slept among them, and surely I feel it possible to die myself as calmly as any,—but enough of this. The fight is now fearful, and ambulances are coming in with great rapidity, each bearing its suffering load.

Fourteen Miles from White House on York River
May 30th, 1864

We are now fourteen miles from Richmond, having marched pretty steadily southward ever since I last wrote. Oh, why will not the Confederacy burst up! True, we are drawing very near to Richmond, but the tug of war will come at the Chickahominy River. Although the Confederates had the shortest road, we rather stole a march upon them this time before they could reach and stop us, and, by making a hard, forced march, we saved many lives. The morale of the enemy is injured by their falling back in retreat so far, while that of our army is correspondingly improved. They are now pretty near their last ditch, and the fight there will be fierce and strong. I work day and night, and when not busy with the sick and wounded am on the tedious march.

Cold Harbor
June 4th, 1864

I have not had a moment to write for nearly a week. It has been fight, fight, fight. Every day there is a fight, and every day the hospital is again filled. For four days now we have been operating upon the men wounded in one battle, which lasted only about two hours; but the wounds were more serious than those from former engagements. I am heartsick over it all. If the Confederates lost in each fight the same number as we, there would be more chance for us; but their loss is about one man to our five, from the fact that they never leave their earthworks, whereas our men are obliged to charge even when there is not the slightest chance of taking them. Several times after capturing these works our troops were unsupported and had to evacuate immediately, with great loss. The men are becoming discouraged, but there is plenty of fight in them yet.

June 7th, 1864

For the first time, I believe, since this campaign commenced, I am lying upon my blankets at twelve o'clock noon. This morning early we sent almost every man in the hospital to the "White House," to make room for others. Under a flag of truce, we asked permission of the enemy to take off our wounded who were lying between the two lines. This, of course, prevented all hostilities, and we surgeons are having a few hours' rest.

June 10th, 1864

The front lines are within thirty yards of the Confederate works,—indeed, so near that a biscuit could easily be tossed into them. On neither side do the men dare show their heads above the entrenchments, for it is almost sure death to do so. The sharpshooters on both sides are so placed that they can pick off anything which appears in sight.

We have had thirty of our division wounded to-day by shell which the Confederates manage to throw into our pits, but we are successful in dropping some into theirs also. The heat is intolerable, and the roads are covered with dust six or eight inches deep, which every gust of wind sweeps up, covering everything with a dirty, white coating.

Field Hospital near Petersburg
June 24th, 1864

I am up to my neck in work. It is slaughter, slaughter. Our
brigade has met with a sad loss by having three entire regiments gobbled up as prisoners. The Twentieth fortunately
escaped. This misfortune was caused by the second brigade
giving way before the attack of the enemy and exposing the
flank of our own. The enemy, before we knew it, was in our
rear, and resistance was absurd. Major Hooper, who commanded the brigade, was the only one of the Fifteenth Massachusetts who escaped. He received a slight wound in the
arm, however, and started for home yesterday. Lucky fellow!
No time for writing more.

June 27th, 1864

When our division was withdrawn from the extreme front,
where it has been since the beginning of the campaign, we
surgeons looked for a little less arduous work; but now the
artillery brigade has been placed under our care, and we have
as much to do as ever. It has not rained for a month, and the
poor wounded fellows lie all about me, suffering intensely
from heat and flies. The atmosphere is almost intolerable from
the immense quantity of decomposing animal and vegetable
matter upon the ground. Many of the surgeons are ill, and
I indulge in large doses of quinine. Horses and mules die by
hundreds from continued hard labor and scant feed. The
roads are strew with them, and the decay of these, with that of
human bodies in the trenches, causes malaria of the worst
kind.

War! War! War! I often think that in the future when human
character shall have deepened, there will be a better way of
settling affairs than this of plunging into a perfect maelstrom
of horror.

Field Hospital
June 29th, 1864

Rumor says that the Twentieth is to be mustered out of service on the 18th of July.

Grant is winding his forces round Petersburg. Our infantry is about two miles from the Weldon Railroad, and it is reported that our cavalry have cut the railroad lower down. The Confederates are close to starvation, especially the women and children, and yet there is no sign of their yielding.

Our division has again been put in the front line of rifle-pits, and again the poor wounded fellows will be coming in. All this accumulation of experience quickly changes careless boys into sober and thoughtful men,—men who trust, and who feel that whatever happens, in the end it will somehow be for the best; men who value what has not cost them a thought before. I know of a little book, carried in breast pocket or knapsack,—indeed, wherever it may seem safest,—that has now become a dependence amid suffering and privation.

July 2nd, 1864

For several days I have had no time to write.

The report to-night is that the Second corps is to take transports for Maryland. This may be true or not. We have few wounded men in the hospital, but a great many sick. However, the army, is on the whole, comparatively healthy.

July 8th, 1864

The Twentieth Massachusetts is to be consolidated into a battalion of seven companies, and an order just issued by the War Department says that officers not having served three years from the last muster will be retained, if needed. According to this order, not an individual officer, except the quartermaster, can be mustered out on the 18th, when the regiment is supposed to go home.

It is intolerably hot, and has been for some time. No rain has fallen since the last of May. Our hospital is now in the woods close to the highway, and we have the benefit of the dust, which so incessantly sweeps over us that we eat and breathe it until almost suffocated by it.

July 18th, 1864

I am retained and General Hancock says I must remain. I may be mustered out of service before very long, however. I know very well that General Hancock from his standpoint is right to retain me, but all the same it seems as if I could not bear it. If I remained in the army until September I should be made surgeon, but I do not care a fig for that now.

Perry, John G., as compiled by Perry, Martha Derby. *Letters from a Surgeon of the Civil War.* Boston: Little, Brown and Company, 1906.

Thirteen Months in the Rebel Army

by *William G. Stevenson*

ON FEBRUARY 13, 1862, Como. Andrew H. Foote, leading the Union fleet, returned to the Ohio River and came up the Cumberland River while Grant crossed overland to cooperate in the capture of Fort Donelson. This large fortress covered more than one hundred acres, crowned a bluff one hundred feet high, and commanded the river for a distance of two miles. On the land side was a line of rifle pits and batteries protected by abatis and interlaced brush, extending along the wooded hills for two and a half miles. The fort mounted sixty-five guns.

Soon after Grant's arrival, Maj. Gen. John A. McClernand led his Union division in an assault on a battery but was repulsed. A bitter storm of hail and snow came on at dusk, and the hardy western troops of the Union lay down in the line of battle without fires or tents, many of them without blankets. The wounded who could not crawl off were left where they had fallen in the narrow space between the two armies, and their piteous cries continued through the night. The next afternoon, the gunboats moved up to within 300 yards of the fort, engaging the water batteries. Heavy fire from the fort hit the Union flagship fifty-nine times and crippled many of the accompanying boats, forcing them to withdraw. Commodore Foote was wounded in the engagement, but the Confederate works were unimpaired, and no one in them was seriously hurt.

Everything had gone against the Union Army up to that time, but reinforcements began to arrive, until the troops numbered between 30,000 and 40,000 men. The Confederates realized their position was growing precarious, with the superior numbers pouring into the field, and they began to despair of a successful defense. It was decided to break through the lines and force a way to Nashville. The next morning, an hour before daybreak, Gen. Gideon J. Pillow moved his forces out against Grant's right wing, while Gen. Simon B. Buckner launched a vigorous attack at the center of the front.

The Confederate forces were successful in their initial rush, and the Wynn's Ferry Road lay open before them. But by some strange quirk, they did not fully seize the object for which they had been fighting. Grant, who had been with the fleet consulting with Commodore Foote, returned to the battlefield, and seeing that a critical moment had arrived, he *ordered a general advance along the whole line. His men swept all before them, recovered the battlefield, and if there had been another half hour of daylight, would have taken Donelson.*

That night the temperature sank to 10 degrees above zero. The troops on both sides, with neither fire nor shelter, shivered in the snowstorm. The ground on which they lay was covered with a sheet of ice. Hundreds of the wounded were strewn in the field, staining the snow crimson, stiffening and freezing as they slowly died.

William G. Stevenson, a frustrated New Yorker pressed into the medical service by the Confederacy, continues the story of the wounded as they came up from Nashville. He wrote Thirteen Months in the Rebel Army *during the war, after he escaped from the Confederate Army.*

I give to you, in the following pages, a simple narrative of facts. I have no motive to misrepresent or conceal. I have an honest desire to describe faithfully and truly what I saw and heard during thirteen months of enforced service in the Rebel army.

If I should seem to you to speak too favorably of individuals or occurrences in the South, I beg you to consider that I give impressions obtained when in the South. If my book has any value it lies in this very fact, that it give you an interior view of this stupendous rebellion, which can not be obtained by one standing in the North and looking at it only with Northern eyes.

I have confidence in truth; and unwelcome truth, is none the less truth, and none the less valuable. Sure am I, that if the North had known the whole truth as to the *power, the unanimity, and the deadly purpose* of the leaders in the rebellion, the government would have been far better prepared for promptly meeting the crisis. Look then candidly at facts, and give them their true weight.

As I am under no obligation, from duty or honor, to conceal what I was compelled to see and hear in the South, I tell it frankly; hoping it may be of value to my bleeding country, I tell it plainly. I have no cause to love the Confederate usurpation, as will fully appear, yet I refrain from abusive and denunciatory epithets, because both my taste and judgment enjoin it.

For the accuracy of names, dates and places, I rely wholly upon memory. I kept memoranda during my whole service, but was compelled to leave everything when I attempted to escape, as such papers then found in my possession would have secured my certain death; but in all material things I can promise the accuracy which a retentive memory secures.

With this brief word, I invite you to enter with me upon the Southern service.

William G. Stevenson
New York City, Sept. 15th, 1863.

The wounded were now arriving in large numbers, but so exhausted by the loss of blood, the jolting in rough wagons, and the exposure of the fearful night, that many were too far gone for relief.

As I had, while at school in New York, frequented the hospitals, and also attended two courses of medical lectures, I had gained a little knowledge of wounds and their treatment. This fact, and a special fondness if not aptitude for that study, decided my future course.

My first care was for the members of the company I had commanded during the long retreat from Nashville; hence I went out to seek them. Meeting them a short distance from Corinth, I had them taken to a hospital established in an unfurnished brick church in the north end of the town, and here I remained, giving them all possible care and attention.

Next morning, Dr. J. O. Nott, Surgeon-general of the Western division of the Confederate service, appointed me as assistant-surgeon on his staff. The scarcity of surgeons to meet the immense demand and, perhaps, a little skill shown in dressing wounds, secured me this appointment. On the following Saturday, April 12, 1862, I obtained an honorable discharge from the army, on account of my wounds, but retained my position of assistant-surgeon, as a civilian appointment.

During the ten days I remained at Corinth the town was a perfect *aceldama*, though all was done that could be to save life and alleviate suffering. Many of the best surgeons in the South arrived in time to render valuable assistance to the army surgeons in their laborious duties. Among these may be named Surrell of Virginia, Hargis and Baldwin of Mississippi, Richardson of New Orleans, La Fressne of Alabama, with many others of high reputation. During the week following the battle the wounded were brought in by hundreds, and the surgeons were over-tasked. Above 5000 wounded men, demanding instant and constant attendance, made a call too great to be met successfully. A much larger proportion of amputations was performed than would have been necessary if the wounds could have received earlier attention. On account of exposure, many wounds were gangrenous when the patients reached the hospital. In these cases delay was fatal, and an operation almost equally so, as tetanus often followed speedily. Where amputation was performed, eight out of ten died. The deaths in Corinth averaged fifty per day for a week after the battle. While the surgeons, as a body, did their duty nobly, there were some young men, apparently just out of college, who performed difficult operations with the assurance and assumed skill of practiced surgeons, and with little regard for human life or limb. In a few days erysipelas broke out, and numbers died of it. Pneumonia, typhoid fever, and measles followed, and Corinth was one entire hospital. As soon as possible, the wounded who could be moved were sent off to Columbus, Okalona, Lauderdale Springs, and elsewhere, and some relief was thus obtained. We were also comforted by the arrival of a corps of nurses. Their presence acted like a charm. Order emerged from chaos, and in a few hours all looked cleaner and really felt better, from the skill and industry of a few devoted women. A pleasant instance of the restraint of woman's presence upon the roughest natures occurred in the hospital I was attending. A stalwart backwoodsman was suffering from a broken arm, and had been venting his spleen upon the doctors and male nurses by continued profanity; but when one of his fellow-sufferers uttered an oath, while the "Sisters" were near ministering to the comfort of the wounded, he sharply reproved him, demanding—"Have you no more manners than to swear in the presence of ladies?" All honor to those devoted Sisters, who, fearless of danger and disease, sacrificed every personal comfort to alleviate the sufferings of the sick and wounded after this terrible battle.

An instance of most heroic endurance, if not of fool-hardy stoicism, such as has few parallels in history, occurred during the contest, which deserves mention. Brigadier-General Gladden, of South Carolina, who was in General Bragg's command, had his left arm shattered by a ball on the first day of the fight. Amputation was performed hastily by his staff-surgeon on the field; and then, instead of being taken to the rear for quiet and nursing, he mounted his horse, against the most earnest remonstrances of all his staff, and continued to command. On Monday, he was again in the saddle, and kept it during the day; on Tuesday, he rode on horseback to Corinth, twenty miles from the scene of action, and continued to discharge the duties of an officer. On Wednesday, a second amputation, near the shoulder, was necessary, when General Bragg sent an aid to ask if he would not be relieved of his command. To which he replied, "Give General Bragg my compliments, and say that General Gladden will only give up his command to go into his coffin." Against the remonstrances of personal friends, and the positive injunction of the surgeons, he persisted in sitting up in his chair, receiving dispatches and giving directions, till Wednesday afternoon, when lockjaw seized him, and he died in a few moments. A sad end was this, for a man possessing many of the noblest and most exalted characteristics.

My purpose to disconnect myself from the South strengthened. If I couldn't get my pay which was now many months in arrears, I could not travel many hundreds of miles without means, and in a direction to excite suspicion in the mind of every man I might meet. But the paymaster was not in funds; and while he approved and indorsed my bills, he said I must go to Richmond to receive the money. I had not means to go to Richmond to receive the money. My horses, of which I owned two, I was determined to keep, to aid me off; hence I was forced to continue my position as assistant-surgeon for a time.

On the 17th of April, the surgeon-general to whose staff I was attached left Corinth for Mobile, nearly three hundred miles distant, with a train conveying about forty wounded men. The journey was tedious, and to the wounded, painful, as they occupied box-cars without springs and the weather was exceedingly warm. A few of the men were left under the care of physicians by the way, being unable to endure the motion of the cars. We proceeded leisurely from station to station, stopping long enough to receive provisions for all on board from the citizens on the line of the road, which were freely and gratuitously furnished. Wherever we stopped long enough to give the people time to assemble, crowds came to offer relief,—ladies with flowers, jellies, and cakes for the poor fellows, and men with the more substantial provisions. One rich old gentleman at Lauderdale Springs named Martin, sent in a wagon loaded with stores. The exuberance of supplies thus voluntarily furnished, is an index of the feeling of the masses in the South as to the cause in which they have embarked their all.

At the end of two and a half days we reached Mobile, and

were met at the depot by a large company of ladies with carriages, to take the wounded men to a spacious and airy hospital,
prepared with every necessary and comfort which could be
devised. A large number of servants were in attendance, to carry
those too severely wounded to ride in the carriages; and whatever water, and clean suits, and food, and smiles, and sympathy,
and Christian conversation, and religious books, could do for
their comfort was done.

After seeing the men nicely cared for, and resting, I set myself
to investigations as to the possibility of escape from Mobile out
to the blockading fleet, in case I could not get my pay to go home
by land. I met no cheering facts in this search. There were about
4000 troops in and around the city. Fort Morgan was strongly
guarded, and egress was difficult, while the Union fleet lay far
out. I gave this up, as not feasible for the present, at least.

Mobile was stagnant commercially, business at a stand-still,
many stores closed, and all looked gloomy. The arrival from
Havana of a vessel which had eluded the blockading fleet,
loaded with coffee, cigars, &c., produced a temporary and feeble
excitement. But so frequent were those arrivals that the novelty
had worn off; though in this fact I see no ground for reproaching
either the heads of department at Washington or the commanders of the blockading squadron at the point. The whole coast is
indented with bays, and interior lines of navigable water are
numerous; so that nothing but a cordon of ships, in close proximity along the whole coast, could entirely forbid ingress and
egress.

Another instance of the rigid surveillance of the press maintained in the Confederate States is suggested by this incident.
The city papers of Mobile made no mention of this arrival,
though all knew it. Early in the year, Southern papers boasted of
the number of ships which accomplished the feat, giving names,
places, and cargoes; but months ago this was forbidden, and
wisely for their interests. Recently I have seen no mention in
Southern papers of the importation of cannon or anything else,
except in purposely blind phrase as to time and place.

I returned to the hospital, feeling that my destinies were
wrapped up with it for a while yet. Here I witnessed an illustra-

tion of the power of popular enthusiasm worthy of mention. A
miserly old gentleman, who had never been known, it was said,
to do a generous act, and who had thrown off all appeals for aid
to ordinary benevolent causes with an imperative negative, was
so overcome by the popular breeze in favor of the soldiers, that
he came into the hospital with a roll of bank-bills in his hand,
and passing from cot to cot gave each wounded man a five-
dollar bill, repeating, with a spasmodic jerk of his head and a
forced smile, "Make yourself comfortable; make yourself comfortable, my good fellow." I am afraid he, poor fellow, did not
feel very comfortable, as his money was screwed out of him by
the power of public opinion.

The Surgeon-General, a man as noble in private life as distin-
guished in his profession, asked me to take charge of a hospital
at Selma, one hundred and eighty miles up the Alabama river,
under the direction of Dr. W. P. Reese, post-surgeon; and on the
21st of April I left for that place,with twenty-three wounded
men under my care. We reached the town the next day, my men
improved by the river transit. Here we were again met by carriages, in readiness to convey the wounded to a hospital, fitted
up in a large Female Seminary building, admirably adapted for
the purpose, with spacious rooms, high ceilings, and well ventilated. One wing of this building, containing a large music room,
was appropriated to my charge. The sick men of a regiment
organizing there, occupied another part of the building. The
school, like so many others in the South, was scattered by the
war.

Here again we were burdened with kindness from the ladies.
Wines, jellies, strawberries, cakes, flowers, were always abundant, served by beautiful women, with the most bewitching
smiles. I had been so long cut off from refined female society,
that I appreciated most profoundly their kind attentions. So
intent were they upon contributing to the comfort of the men
who had been wounded in protecting their homes, as they
regarded it, that they brought a piano into my ward, and the
young ladies vied with each other in delectating us with
the Marseillaise, Dixie, and like patriotic songs, interspersing
occasionally something about moonlight walks in Southern

bowers, &c., which my modesty would not allow me to suppose
had any reference to the tall young surgeon.

Selma is a beautiful town of three or four thousand inhabitants, situated on the right bank of the Alabama river, on a level
plateau, stretching off from the bank, which rises from forty to
fifty feet above the river by a steep ascent. A distinguishing fea-
ture of the place is its Artesian wells, said to be equal to any in
the world. In the main street of the town, at the crossing of other
streets, are reservoirs, five in number, which receive the water
thrown up from a depth of many hundred feet, and in quantity
far beyond the demands of the inhabitants. The water is slightly
impregnated with mineral qualities, is pleasant to the taste, and
regarded as medicinal. The people of Selma are generally highly
intelligent and refined and no more pleasant acquaintances did I
form in the South than here. Their zeal for the Rebel cause was
up to fever heat, and their benevolence for its soldiers without
stint. The provisions for the hospital were furnished gratuitously
by a committee of the Relief Association, and they appeared
grieved that we made no more demands upon them. That my
hospital was a model of neatness and perfection in its line, was
attested by a report of Adjutant-General Cooper, who visited
incognito the hospitals through the South while I was at Selma.
He gave it the preference over all he had seen, in a publication
which appeared shortly after this time in the Southern papers.

At the end of three weeks of attendance here, I obtained a furlough for ten days, that I might go to Richmond to secure my
pay. Securing government transportation, I reached Richmond
on the 15th of May, exceedingly anxious to find the quartermaster in an amiable mood and in funds; for upon my success
here depended my hopes of a speedy escape. Money will often
accomplish what daring would not. But here I was disap-
pointed—at least partially. I secured but one-fifth of my claim,
which was admitted without question; but I was told that the
quartermaster of the Western division had funds, and I must get
the remainder there. My remonstrances availed nothing, and I
left the office in no amiable mood.

I now determined to avenge myself upon a faithless government, by acquiring all possible information of the *status* of the

Rebel army in and about Richmond, which might be of use to me and my country. In this I also failed, from the exceeding and, I must say, wise vigilance of the authorities. My pass to enter the city allowed nothing further—I must procure one to remain in the city, and this was called for at almost every street corner; and then another to leave the city, and only in one direction.

Although I appeared in the dress of an assistant-surgeon, with the M.S. upon my cap, I could gain no access to the army outside of the city, nor make any headway in my tour of observation; and as they charged me five dollars per day at the Ballard House, I must soon leave, or be swamped. I had not been so completely foiled in my plans hitherto.

I left Richmond for Selma on the 20th of May, reflecting bitterly upon the character of a rebellion which, commenced in fraud, was perpetuating itself by forcing its enemies to fight their own friends, and then refused to pay them the stipulated price of their enforced service. The longer I reflected, the more fully was I convinced that I never would receive my pay. The conscription act, which took effect the 10th of May, was being enforced with a sweeping and searching universality. If I returned to Corinth to seek the quartermaster there, the payment would be deferred, from one excuse or another, until I should be forced into the service again. The thought that the Rebel authorities were breaking their pledges to pay me, that they might get their hated coils around me once more, from which I had but partially extricated myself, almost maddened me. I know, moreover, that I could not long remain in Selma, in my present situation. The men were all recovering, except one poor fellow, who soon passed beyond the reach of earthly mutilations, and no new shipments of wounded were coming on. And the force of public opinion in Selma was such, that no man able to fight could remain there. The unmarried ladies were so patriotic, that every able-bodied young man was constrained to enlist. Some months previous to this, a gentleman was known to be engaged for an early marriage, and hence declined to volunteer. When his betrothed, a charming girl and a devoted lover, heard of his refusal, she sent him, by the hand of a slave, a package inclosing a note. The package contained a lady's skirt and crinoline, and the note these terse words: "Wear these, or volunteer." He volunteered.

When will the North wake up to a true and manly patriotism in the defense of their national life, now threatened by the tiger-grasp of the atrocious Rebellion? Hundreds upon hundreds of young men I see in stores and shops, doing work that women could do quite as well; and large numbers of older men who have grown wealthy under the protection of our benign government, are idly grieving over the taxation which the war imposes, and meanly asking if it will not soon end, that their coffers may become plethoric of gold; while the question is still unsettled whether the Rebellion shall sweep them and their all into the vortex of ruin and anarchy. *The North is asleep! and it will become the sleep of death, national death, if a new spirit be not speedily awaked!*

Stevenson, William G. *Thirteen Months in the Rebel Army*. New York: A. S. Barnes & Burr, 1863.

The Army of the Potomac – Behind the Scenes

by *Alfred L. Castleman*
Surgeon
5th Regiment of Wisconsin
Volunteers

IN MARCH 1862 Gen. George McClellan was removed as Federal general in chief but was retained to command the Army of the Potomac, whose sole purpose at that time was to protect the Capital from invasion.

The general, thirty-five years old, was excellent in drawing up plans, training an army, and instilling discipline. He built a large, well-equipped army, and the South suddenly became aware of the oversized, efficient force. As time went on, and the pressure upon the Capital by the rebel army was reduced, President Lincoln looked to McClellan to move his army into battle, but the general was reluctant. A born procrastinator, he put off the president until leading federal politicians urged Lincoln to order McClellan to move his troops to the battlefield.

A surgeon in this Army of the Potomac, Alfred L. Castleman, wrote about his experiences in the idle army. His frustration at the petty bickering and the bureaucracy he encountered changed the face of the treatment he could afford the troops. Castleman, a dedicated man, tasted small-minded grievances and obstruction that blunted his loyalty and dedication to the cause before the troops moved into battle.

The following introduction appeared in Castleman's original work. In the Milwaukee Sentinel newspaper of July 27, 1863, a book reviewer wrote:

> We have seen and had the chance to peruse the greater portion of the work in sheets, and can speak of it understandingly. In his preface, the author says: "The record having been made for the writer is, for the most part, confined to a statement of such things as are not written in histories;" and also as will be noticed by the title page, it purports to be a look `behind the scenes.' These statements truly indicate its character, and insure its interest to the reader. The current partial history of the war all readers are familiar with, and for a perfect accurate history, of course, the time has not yet come. This work furnishes what the newspapers have never given, and what no history of the war will ever pick up.

It is a dash at all the salient, interesting points of a military life, through the most interesting and eventful period of the history of the Potomac army, written in a style, easy, flowing, and in itself attractive. And, besides its reference to passing events, the opinions of the author, touching the men, McClellan among the chief, who have led and figured prominently in the Potomac army, given evidently without "fear, favor, affection or the hope of reward," are valuable as the candid views of an intelligent observing man, with the data on which to form an opinion.

The book, besides its general interest, has a local interest to all Wisconsin readers, and especially those particularly interested in the 5th Wisconsin. We can most cheerfully recommend it as a book of much more than ordinary interest and value of the present time.

January 2, 1862.—I think my hospital can boast, just now, the happiest set of sick men I ever saw. I have now twenty-seven of them. This morning, as I was prescribing for them, (all sitting up) some reading the morning papers, and talking loudly over war news, some playing whist, some checkers, some chess, some dominoes—all laughing and merry, Gen. H——walked in, and, looking for a moment along the line of sick, exclaimed, "What the h——ll have you got here?"

"My hospital, General."

"A Brigade," replied he in his roughest manner, "of a d——d sight better men than you have left me. Where are your sick, sir?"

"All here, sir."

"Well, this beats anything I have seen in the army, and if you give your men such beds and such comforts as this, you will have every man of your regiment in hospital before a month."

They have had a glorious holiday. The boxes, and other presents received within the last eight days, have awakened vivid recollections of home, and of "the girls they left behind them." They are all the better for these things, and when I return them to their quarters, they take hold of their work with a will, and with a feeling that if taken sick, they have a pleasant hospital to go to.

I make here a record of some observations in relation to "hospital fever," "hospital sores," "foul air of hospitals," and such clap-trap. I have lately visited many tent hospitals, in the open field, where I have witnessed cases of "hospital gangrene," low typhoid fevers, with gangrenous toes or fingers dropping off, and heard scientific men in scientific discussions, attributing it all to the foul air of the hospital! And this, too, in the open field, where not more than thirty or forty were together, and where the wind swept past them, free as the fresh breezes on the top of the Alleghanies!! `Twas a gangrene of the mind, for want of free ventilation of the brain. There is no disease so contagious, or so depressing to vital energy when taken, as inactivity and gloominess of mind. Introduce one such temperament into your hospital, *without an accom-*

panying antidote, and the condition will be communicated to all others in the hospital, with as much certainty, and with greater rapidity, than would the infection of small-pox or measles. Let the admission of such a patient be accompanied by the presence of a long, sour-faced hospital steward, who keeps in the hospital tent a table covered with cups, and spoons, and vials, and pill-boxes, and syringes, and who mingles with every potion he gives a homily on hospital sickness, on fatality in the army, on the number of deaths from typhoid in the next tent, and my word and observation for it, though the breezes of that hospital come fresh "from Greenland's icy mountains," they will be freighted with the mephite vapors of hospital fever and gangrene.

Instead of the above, let the Surgeon pass frequently through his hospital, making it a rule never to leave till he has elicited a hearty laugh from every one in it. For his Steward's table of mirth-repelling instruments, introduce light reading, chess-men, checkers, dominoes, cards, puzzles, their use to be regulated by a corps of jolly, mirth loving, but judicious nurses. Then let him throw up the bottoms of his tent walls, giving everything around an air of cheerfulness, and if he does not find the diseases of the field hospital milder and more tractable than at home, my word for it, it will be in consequence of the officious overdosing by the doctor. I do not mean that cleanliness is not an essential; but I must bear in mind that a pile of nasty, out-of-place rubbish, is as incompatible with cheerfulness, as it is with purity of surrounding air. A clean bed, even, exhilarates the mind, as promptly as it corrects the foul odors of a soiled one. Since I have been in the army, I have lost all dread of the much-talked-of foul air of hospitals, *only so far as it is difficult to correct the mental atmosphere about it.* This is in reference to its influence on diseases. I have not yet had an opportunity of observing the effects of crowds *in surgical* wards—that will come before long, and I shall be greatly relieved if I find the same records applicable there.

5th.—I am very hard worked just now. The Brigade Surgeon is sick, and I being the ranking Surgeon in the Brigade, have his duties to perform. In addition, I have charge, at present, of a large share of the Hospital of the 49th Regiment Penn. Vols, the Surgeon being very ill. That regiment is in dreadful condition. Very many of them are sick, and of very grave diseases. Then, my assistant is off of duty, being suspended on account of charges pending against him, in court martial. From altogether I am much worn down, and need rest.

In my own Regiment, I have none who can be properly called *sick*. I excuse 75 to 100 from duty almost every day, but it is chiefly on account of bad colds, chaffed feet, or some minor trouble. I have not one man confined *to bed*, from sickness.

There are many dark clouds hanging over the country now. Amongst them, there are evident signs of loss of confidence in Gen. McClellan. I hope he will make haste to give good account of himself, and thus regain the confidence he has lost.

7th.—This has been a cold, blustry day, and the Regiment has been out skirmishing. They found no enemy; bought a little corn, and came home.

All is conjecture here as to the intention of our leaders. My conjecture is that outside pressure will compel us to do something within the next fifteen days or lose still more confidence. But what can we do? Nothing here. The roads are impracticable for artillery—the weather too bad to fight. If we do anything we must go south. I am getting very tired of this, and wish I could feel that it would be proper for me to resign.

18th.—I visited Washington to-day, through such rain and such mud, as no civilized country, save this, can sustain, and preserve its character for purity. Am back tonight. On my return, I find on my table the following:

"General Order No. 11

"Headquarters, &c.

"When the time arrives for the troops of this Brigade
to move, the following will be the allowance of the means of
transportation:

"Five wagons to the companies of a Regiment (two wagons
to each company); one wagon to the Regimental Hospital.

"Each wagon will carry the forage for its horses. The sixty
rounds of reserved ammunition will be carried in extra wagons. In the company wagons, will be carried rations for two or
three days, company mess equipage, and officers' baggage,
which will in no case exceed the amount by regulations for
baggage in the field. The forage for horses of regimental and
field officers will have to be carried in their wagons. This
notice is given so that soldiers and officers may be aware, that
all property not above mentioned, to be preserved, had better
be removed, for if the troops march, it is probable the first
notice given will be the presence of wagons for loading.

"By order of Brig. Gen ———."

Now that begins to look like business, and if our General
means to put us in the way of doing something—if it will only
not prove another counterfeit cry of "wolf"—we shall be
pleased. Gen. McClellan has already grown several inches in
the estimation of those whose confidence began to get shaky. I
do not like the expression of "for if the troops march." It
looks a little wolfy. But I shall try to think it means "go in."

19th.—I confess to myself to-night, that deeply as I am interested in the cause for which we fight—the question of government against anarchy—what I have witnessed to-day has
cooled much of the enthusiasm with which I entered the service of the government, which I find so tardy in doing justice
to those who are fighting for its preservation. This is a stormy
day in mid-winter. Whilst going my rounds of camp to see
what was needed for the health and comfort of the men, I
passed the guard house of the regiment, and stepped in to see

the condition of things. I there found soldiers—formerly my neighbors—sons of my friends, imprisoned in a *pen* where pigs could not have lived a fortnight without scalding the hair off them, (this is not figurative language) and in which these men had been kept for three months awaiting the decision of a court martial which had tried them for some trivial offence, the extremest penalty of which would have amounted to some three to six days confinement! at all events, under the extremest limit of the law, its punishment could not have exceeded in severity a sentence of three days' imprisonment in this vile hole of filth and water! Yes, they had been tried, and for three months had been kept, not only in this vile hole, but under indignity and disgrace, awaiting the convenience of gentlemanly officers, to send them word whether they were honorably acquitted, or that they must be imprisoned for two or three days. When these men, who, perhaps, have never been guilty of offence besides being suspected of it, are released from this disgraceful punishment, will they not feel indignant at hearing the justice of their government questioned and be ready to rush to arms again to defend it? If scenes like this are *necessary* to the preservation of a government for my protection, then in God's name let *me* be untrammelled by conventional forms, and left dependent on my own powers for my protection. I assumed a prerogative; I pronounced most of these men sick, and ordered them sent to my hospital. They will hardly be pronounced well before the gentlemanly members of the court get ready to inform them of their sentence.

From this last scene I passed on to look up a party of our Regiment, who had been detailed to guard the General's headquarters. I found them; and, my God! what a sight!— Around the house occupied by the General was a large ditch, some five feet deep, and some ten or twelve feet wide, dug as the commencement of a fort. In this ditch, over which a few evergreen boughs had been thrown as a covering, stood a well dressed Lieutenant, (from my own county) with a squad of soldiers guarding the General's house—the Lieutenant trying to infuse into the men a little warmth of patriotic feeling, whilst the winter torrents poured through the evergreen branches, and their whole frames shook with cold in this *sentry house*, charitably built for them by orders of the General who at that moment was being joyful over his wine, and with his friends!! And is this the REPUBLIC, the government of equality for which I am fighting! If we were *men*, this would be pitiable, but we are only soldiers, volunteer soldiers at that; and what right have we to be cold, when our services are wanted for the comfort of a General? But these are only *thoughts;* should I write or speak them, it would amount to shameful insubordination, and I should be disgracefully dismissed from the service of the country which tolerates it. I am too honorable a man to permit myself to be disgraced, even for the privilege of uttering a truth. I therefore decline to say, or even to write, what I have seen.

This afternoon I received an order to be ready to move at a moment's notice, and to give no more certificates for furloughs, as the applications would not be entertained. I have lost faith in the idea that the authorities have the slightest intention to move. They have seen our impatience to do something, and this order is a mere dumb-watch thrown us children to amuse us with the old promised hope that "when it gets a little older it will keep time."

23rd.—The whole atmosphere to-night vibrates with the sounds of preparation to advance. The new Secretary of War says "advance." We are getting daily dispatches from Gen. McClellan, asking, "Are you ready?" I have no faith. We have received too many dumb-watches, which "will run when they get older."

27th.—Expectation is still on the strain. How long it has been kept up! But no order to move, and I doubt whether we get any soon. Indeed, I think now that we should not move. 'Tis too late. The roads are excessively bad, and for a long time we have been having an almost continuous storm of freezing rain and snow. An army could not lie out every night in this terrible weather, and be in condition next day to fight against those who had slept in good quarters and been well fed. The time has passed to move. But why are we not ordered to winter quarters? There seems to me to be great recklessness of the soldiers' health and comfort in this army. There is wrong somewhere.

A sad case has just passed under my notice. Three days ago, as I was busily engaged in attending to hospital duties, I entrusted, necessarily, the light sickness of quarters to others. As I passed out just after morning call, I heard one of my nurses say to a man, "You look sick; why do you not come to hospital, where we can take care of you?"

"That is what I came for, but the doctor says I am not sick, and has returned me *to duty.*"

I passed on, but notwithstanding that there is scarcely a day that some "shirk" who is pretending to be sick to avoid duty, is not treated thus, that voice rang sadly in my ears. In ten minutes I returned, and inquired after the man. The drums had beaten to duty, and he was on parade. I followed to parade ground, found him endeavoring to do his duty, on a "double-quick." I took him from the ranks, examined him, and sent him to hospital. Before they got him to bed he was delirious. He has just died. 'Twas a case of typhoid fever, of which he had been sick for two days before I saw him. I ask of army Surgeons, had you not better excuse ten "seeds" who are worthless, even when in rank, than sacrifice one good man like this, who believes he is not sick, *because you tell him he is not?*

February 7th.—Still all is uncertainty here as to what is in store for us. Some are of opinion that we are to accompany the next squadron to the South; some that we go to Norfolk; others that we shall next week move on Manassas. My own opinion is that we shall remain where we are till about the first of April, then advance on Centreville, and if successful to Manassas, and thus to follow up our victories as long as we can win them.

Today our Regiment is scouting. This morning a body of Cavalry went out from our Brigade, and returned about ten o'clock, bringing in six rebel cavalry men as prisoners. But some of our own men are missing. We immediately sent out two regiments to reconnoitre. They have returned with thirteen prisoners. Two of the Cameron Dragoons are wounded, but not badly.

9th.—The Court of Inquiry to examine into the conduct of my hospital affairs yesterday, decided that they would not investigate—that the accusations were the result of personal ill feelings. At least, so a member of the court informed me. I begged him to insist on an inquiry, and the court has reconsidered its action and will investigate. I hope there will be a full *expose* of the whole conduct of the hospital. I have long desired it.

15th.—What a week of news, opening on us with intelligence of the capture of Fort Henry, with its list of high-bred prisoners. Scarcely had the sound of the cheers and the hurrahs died away, when Burnside startled us with an artillery discharge of news. To-day, whilst we were brushing out our "hollering organs" with alum swabs, when the startling intelligence from Fort Donelson, the most glorious of which is the capture of arch-traitor, Floyd;[1] and what a disappointment that not a throat in our whole Division can shout "Hang him!" loud enough for Floyd to hear it. Hold one for awhile, and send us no more such news at present. As this poor old "grandmother" of armies is to do no fighting, wait at least till the

---

[1] John Buchanan Floyd, an attorney who was rewarded for his efforts in the Buchanan election with a cabinet post as Secretary of War (1857-1860), resigned because of his dispute over Union Maj. Robert Anderson's removal from Fort Moultrie. President Buchanan in the meantime had requested his resignation because of irregular and unauthorized practices in the War Department, which involved an apparent loss of $87,000. Feeling was bitter in the North, for a belief persisted that he had transferred large quantities of arms to the South. He served as a Confederate general, but because of his incompetence, he was finally relieved of his command after his defeat at Fort Donelson.

throats of our soldiers so far recover that they can do the shouting over victories in which they are denied the privilege of participating. We have lain still here till we have grown into old fogyism—gone to seed. So little advance, so little progress have we made, within the memory of any here, that should Methuselah offer us to-day a shake of his hand, we should wonder whether it was yesterday or a week ago that we parted from him, so little has been the change *here* since his advent, and so much would he look like all around him.

21st.—This morning Brigade Surgeon ———, of ——— Brigade, made the following statement on the investigation of my hospital management and condition: "I was Surgeon of a Regiment in the three months service; since then I have been Brigade Surgeon of four Brigades;" (including 18 regiments) "I have seen no hospital fund anywhere as large as that of this hospital; I have seen none managed with more economy, nor any patients made so comfortable. I have seen no Surgeon anywhere who seemed to feel so lively an interest in the hospital and the welfare of his regiment; I have seen no Surgeon who devoted so many hours in the service of the sick, as this Surgeon."

This statement, coming officially from a Surgeon whose duty it has been to supervise the care of the hospitals and the treatment of the sick; from an officer whose business has for the last ten months brought him in contact with half the hospitals of the army of the Potomac, and whose headquarters have been for several months within sixty feet of my hospital, was gratifying to me, and entirely satisfactory to those whose duty it was made to investigate, and they so expressed themselves in dismissing the subject.

26th.—A pleasant little interlude to-day, to the troubles and hard work through which I have had to pass: At about twelve o'clock, a soldier stepped to the door of my quarters, and said that some friends wished to see me at the door. I stepped out and found my whole corps of hospital attendants, and the patients of the hospital who were able to be up, in a circle. The head nurse stepped forward, and in a very neat little speech, presented me, in the name of himself and the others, a very pretty regulation dress sword and belt. I replied to it as well and as appropriately as I could; the ceremony closed by a vociferous testimonial of kind feelings, and we parted. I confess that I have been highly gratified. The compliment was appreciated by the fact that it came directly from those who most intimately know me, both personally and officially.

27th.—Three days ago we received orders again to be ready to move at a moment's warning. But here we are yet. I was in Washington to-day. Went intending to spend two days and witness the "doings of Congress." But on my arrival got intelligence that Gen. Banks had crossed the Potomac at Edward's Ferry; that the Government had seized the Railroads here, and was sending off troops to his aid, and not doubting that this would start us also, I immediately returned to my post.

28th.—All the stirring news of yesterday did not uproot us. I begin to think that we are so deeply stuck in the mud that nothing can get us out, short of the sight of a rebel. That might galvanize us into a move.

This morning we received an order countermanding the last one to be ready, so that we are again unready. This is the last day of winter, and the coldest we have had. It snows and blows, and this is probably the reason of the countermand.

March 3d.—In the way of petty tyranny, it seems another Richmond has entered the field. Last week I was presented by some of my friends with a very pretty sword, as a testimonial of their respect and affection for me. To-day I am informed by General ——— that this cannot be tolerated. All the persecution which he and his satellites have heaped on me, have not been sufficient to alienate the affections of those for whom and with whom I have labored for the good of the regiment; but all those who have had any part in the presentation of the sword are to be punished and this, too, at a time when all ranks, from Corporals to Major Generals, are receiving like testimonials! But (?) the head of this Brigade having failed to crush a Surgeon, aspires to a personal quarrel with privates and nurses. Magnanimous General! I have received a positive order, to-day, to ascertain the names of all who had any hand in the presentation of the sword, and to report them to head-quarters, and I have just as positively refused to stoop to participate in any such dirty work. I leave all the honor to the Brigadier General, and after he has vented his malice on such of the privates as he can get other tools to hunt out for him, he is at liberty to try his hand on me again for this disobedience of his dirty order. The work is worthy of him, and the tools he employs.

4th.—I returned from Washington to-day, and was met by Colonel ———, who told me that the Brigade Commander had ordered him to have every hospital nurse who had taken any part in the purchase or presentation of the sword to me, dismissed from hospital and returned to the ranks. Well, now, who is to do that? I shall not; and I am glad that our Commander of Brigade has had pride enough to rise to this trick to find out who they are, rather, than (pencil in hand) to go sneaking around, asking "Who did it?" But he will miss fire, I shall dismiss nobody. I would rather he would catch himself in the act of nosing around for information. I doubt not he will do it, or even dirtier work, rather than let slip any opportunity to gratify his vindictiveness.

After I received this verbal order, I sat down, and wrote a defiant letter to the General, giving him my estimate of such doings, but then, feeling that it might redound to the injury of my friends, who were sharing his displeasure with me, I sup-pressed it, and sent a request to the General to be permitted to see him on the subject. I received the manly reply: "When the

order is carried out!" If we never meet till *I* carry out that
order, these eyes will for a long time be relieved of performing
a most disagreeable duty. He may perform the duty, I shall
not. In the hope, however, of relieving my friends from
his further vindictiveness, I determined on another attempt to
mollify, and here record the attempt, with its result:

> Headquarters Medical Department
> ——— Reg't ——— Vols.

Colonel:

Permit me, through you, to lay before Brigadier General
———, the following statement of facts: During the autumn
and early part of the winter, the sickness in our regiment was
unusually severe. Often, one half of our nurses were sick, and
the rest worn down by fatigue. Rather than draw more
strength from the regiment to our aid, I, after my official
duties of the day were over, did, for weeks together, spend the
greater part of every night in the unofficial, and perhaps,
undignified capacity of nurse, sending the exhausted nurses
to their beds, and ministering to the wants of the sick. I rarely
retired before two o'clock in the morning. During this time I
was so fortunate as to gain the affection and gratitude of those
for whom I labored, whilst many of them were still feeble,
scarcely able to leave their beds, they decided to express their
gratitude for my personal efforts, by a new year's gift to me.
They forgot that in becoming soldiers they ceased to be men,
and gave vent to their feelings by presenting me a sword. If,
in this presentation, there were "deliberations or discussions
having the object of conveying praise or censure" for me, officially, as stated by the General, I have not been able to discover it. The circumstances attending—the spirit of the
address—the inscription on the scabbard all point to a different feeling and another object. With feelings of the deepest
regret, I learn that this act of theirs meets the disapproval of
the Brigade Commander, and that these men are to become
the objects of censure and punishment.

For six months, these soldiers by the direction of the Medical Director of the Army, have been thoroughly trained to the performance of those duties which are expected of hospital attendants on the field of battle, and I venture nothing in saying that the hospital under their care will show that they are second to no corps on the Potomac.

Under the state of facts, I respectfully appeal to the Brigade Commander, and beg that he will revoke the order dismissing these nurses and filling the hospital with inexperienced ones, at the moment when we are expecting to enter the battle field, and to need all the experience in our reach.

I waive all considerations of my own mortification, and will even cheerfully bear a public reprimand for myself. I put aside the consideration of the inconvenience which their dismissal will bring on me; I put aside even *their* mortification and disappointment; but, in behalf of the sick, the wounded, the dying of my regiment, I appeal for the revocation of this order.

> I beg, Sir, to remain,
> Respectfully, your ob't serv't
>
> ———— ————
>
> Surgeon ——— Volunteers

To Colonel ———, Commanding ——— Vols.

With this last appeal I close the labors of this day.

5th.—The deed is done. The blood-hounds tracked out at least a part of their game. The following will tell its own tale:

> Headquarters ——— Reg't ——— Vols
> Camp Griffin, Virginia, March 5th, 1862

Regimental Order
No. 72
Privates ——— ———, ——— ———, ——— ———,
——— ———, ——— ———,[2] are detailed for extra duty

---

[2] (Original author's note) Names of seven privates.

in the Regimental Hospital. They will report to the Surgeon at the hospital forthwith, taking with them their knapsacks, arms, accoutraments, but no ammunition.

Privates ———— ————, ———— ————, ———— ————, ———— ————,[3] are relieved from extra duty at the Regimental Hospital, and will report for duty forthwith, to their company commanders.

The above changes in the attaches of the hospital is deemed necessary, on account of the late complimentary presentation made by the attendants now relieved to the Surgeon in charge of the hospital. This was in violation of the spirit of the army regulations, and of the usage of the service.[4] Yet it is believed that in so doing the men were guilty of no intentional wrong, and were actuated by the better impulses of human nature; and there is, too, much reason to believe that they have been misled by the precedents which have been but too many in the volunteer service. While it is not intended to disgrace the soldiers above named, it is considered that by making this present to their superior in the Medical Department, they have so embarrassed their relationship to that officer as to render the continuance of that relationship subversive of military discipline.

The relationship of officers and soldiers is that of instruction and command on the one part, and of respect and obedience on the other. All discipline is based upon this theory, and while the officer will receive in his own consciousness of duty discharged, and the disinterested approval of his superiors and peers, his sufficient reward, the soldier, by doing his duty in the defence of his country, will continually pay a greater compliment, and make a more acceptable presentation to his officer than handiwork can fashion or money can buy.

By order of the Colonel Commanding,

———— ———— ————, Adjutant

Copy, Official

———— ———— ————, Adjutant.

---

[3] (Original author's note) Names of ten of the hunted out.

[4] (Original author's note) Everybody knows that statement to be false. 'Twas perfectly in accordance with the usage at that time and is yet.

Well, there is a good deal of rhetorical high-fa-lu-tin in all that; but after it shall have been laughed at, hooted and ridiculed by all who see it, I wonder how much comfort the poor soldier who has had his hip shattered or his spine dislocated by a shell, will derive from the recollection of this rhetorical sophistry, whilst he is being handled on the battle field as a bear would handle him, instead of by those hands which had for months been trained to a knowledge of the business, and now withheld for the gratification of a cowardly vindictiveness.

But take it all in all, the above is a remarkable document. Nothing recognized but *order and obedience.* Affection for the commander is entirely ignored. It has been my boast and pride, that for months, not one of the ten men taken from me has been ordered. Their affection for me has anticipated my every wish as well as every necessity of the sick, and there has been a constant emulation amongst them as to who could best please me by contributing to the comforts of the sick. *This, it seems, is not consistent with the good of the service, and they are all this day returned to the ranks!* Well, if military discipline ignores the impulses of affection, and of obedience from kindness, God deliver me from all such drill.

6th.—This morning as my newly appointed nurses came in, I was utterly disheartened. There is not a man amongst them who can make a toast or broil a chicken; yet the sick must depend on them for all their cooking. Half of them are applicants for discharge on the ground of disability, yet they are sent to me to work over the sick, night and day, and to carry the wounded from the battle field. Not one has ever dispensed a dose of medicine, and yet I must depend on them for this duty. It is a dreadful thought to me that I must go to the battle field with the set which is now around me. Our sick, our wounded, our dying on the battle field will be from amongst my neighbors and my friends. To the parents of many I have made a solemn vow that their sons shall be properly cared for in times of trouble. Well, I will do the best I can, but when I have trained men to all the little offices of kindness and of care, even to the practice of lifting the wounded and carrying them smoothly on litters,[5] it is hard that they should now be taken from me, at the very moment of expected battle, and replaced by such as *these*.

This morning the men dismissed from my service for the heinous offence of loving me, came in to bid me good bye. When a long time hence, I read this, I find it written that we all wept, I may then feel ashamed of the weakness. I certainly do not now.

7th.—Received orders to-day to draw rations for my hospital force for five days. This kind of an order is unusual. The roads are improving. Perhaps the dumb watch is nearly old enough to run.

9th.—All is bustle and confusion. Though there is no order to move, we are all packing, and ambulances are running with our sick to general hospital. This looks like clearing the decks for action. We are notified that when we do march, we shall do so without baggage or tents. So long have we been here that, notwithstanding we have been long impatient to move, it will be like breaking up our home. My home attachments are very strong. I shall feel sadly at breaking up, but I shall be glad to be again in active service.

Since the late ebullition of vindictiveness by Gen. ———, I have been schooling myself in the hardest lesson of my life— that is to sit and wait for orders, regardless of humanity, of everything indeed, except the little eighty-seven dollars and fifty cents per month, and my own ease and comfort. This is a lofty ambition. A prize worthy of a better patriot than I have ever claimed to be. Last night and this morning I labored in my hospital till three A.M. But that work is now over. We leave behind us those to whom my care and their suffering

---

[5] (Original author's note) For months, it has been a daily practice to take the nurses to the field and train them to lifting the sick and wounded, and even to the proper step in carrying them off the field. None but those who have witnessed it can imagine the difference in pain or comfort, which a certain kind of step will communicate to those carried on litters.

had attached me; and I will see to it that neither conscience nor humanity shall again so strongly attach me to the sick. It only lays me liable to indignities and insults.

March 10th.—Returned early last night; but before midnight received orders to have two days' rations cooked, and be ready to move at 4 o'clock this A.M. Before I got dressed I found myself not only Regimental Surgeon, but in consequence of the absence of the Brigade Surgeon, I had charge of his duties also. My hands were full. I guess the watch is almost old enough.

We know nothing as to where we *go*, but a party of scouts who were out through the day yesterday, report that Manassas is evacuated, and that the rebel army of the Potomac has all gone South. Almost ten o'clock to day we heard a terrible explosion, supposed to be the blowing up of some bridge to prevent pursuit. And has that army been so disrespectful to General McClellan as to go off without going into his bag? Fie on them!

And now we are off. The sick whom I have nursed till my care grew into affection for them, are sent away. Those to come will be new ones. The last few weeks have taught me that in the army the Surgeon's duty is to take care of the Surgeon, and to leave conscience and humanity to take care of themselves. These, with the affections which are apt to accompany them, may be good enough in civil life; in the army they are obsolete, fit only for fogies. True, there are a few yet in the Regiment, for whom, should they be suffering, I might yield to the sheepish impulse of humanity, and even become interested in their comfort. But Surgeon—first, is to be my motto now. Hurrah! we are on the move!

Castleman, Alfred L. *The Army of the Potomac—Behind the Scenes.* Milwaukee: Strickland & Co., 1863.

A Confederate Surgeon's Letters to His Wife

by Spencer Glasgow Welch
Surgeon
13th South Carolina Volunteers,
McGowan's Brigade

DURING MAY 1862, "Stonewall" Jackson conducted a brilliant campaign in the Shenandoah Valley. This campaign, while inconclusive in itself, weakened the Northern effort in the Peninsular Campaign as Federal forces were withdrawn from that area to oppose Jackson.

In the unsuccessful Peninsular Campaign (April-August 1862), Gen. George McClellan attempted to take the Confederate capital at Richmond. The campaign was marked by battles at Yorktown, Seven Pines, and particularly, the Seven Days Battles.

In anticipation of battles to come, the Confederate Army was adding to its medical personnel in the area. One of the surgeons newly arrived was young Dr. Welch, recently married but a volunteer because of his passionate belief in the Confederate cause.

Dr. Welch, attended by his personal slave, endured many hardships with the men in the field, but there seemed to be a loose medical chain of command. Doctors did not keep up with the troops, and medical supplies had trouble meeting up with the doctors. The wounded lay on the battlefield, gathered in long after the fighting stopped. Aside from amputations and doses of morphine, medical help was denied the wounded until they reached hospitals in the rear.

The chaos of Southern military medicine at the beginning of the Civil War pervades the letters the young doctor wrote to his wife. The letters that follow are only a few from a collection that was preserved by the surgeon's daughter, Eloise Welch. They have been edited to omit personal matter.

Near Fredericksburg, Va.
May 16, 1862

I arrived here this morning about ten o'clock. My trip was all
very pleasant, except when I passed through Petersburg and
Richmond—both those places are so crowded. The citizens of
the latter place are greatly alarmed for fear their city will be
captured.

We are close to the enemy now, but there is no certainty of
our having a big fight soon. Captain Hunt's men shot at the
Yankees this morning while on picket duty. The report about
our losing ten men is true. The Yankee cavalry came across
the Rappahannock River and captured them.

Our regiment moved after I arrived to-day and we are now
near Summit station in a place where the chinquapin bushes
are very thick. The regiments are moved every two or three
days to give them practice in moving quickly. All the tents
have been taken away from the men, and that, together with
the change of climate from the coast of South Carolina to
this place, has caused much sickness in our regiment. I will
sleep in the medicine tent, a very comfortable place.

It is bedtime now. I will try to write you a longer letter
next time. The thought of you and our little George makes me
happy, even though I am away off here in Old Virginia.

Hanover County, Va.
May 27, 1862

We have just finished a forced march of about forty miles, and
have fallen back from near Fredericksburg to within ten miles
of Richmond. The Yankees intended to take the Richmond
and Potomac Railroad, so we came to reinforce the army
already stationed here.

We started last Saturday about dark and continued to travel
over the bad, muddy roads all night. We had a very tedious

march and did not stop except to get the artillery out of the mire, and at one time to eat and rest a little. Whenever the men would come to mud holes and fords of rivers they would plunge right in without hesitating a moment. This is necessary, because an army must never be allowed to hesitate at anything.

Our brigade consists of the Twelfth, Thirteenth and Fourteenth South Carolina and the Thirty-eighth North Carolina regiments, and is commanded by General Maxey Gregg.

Our division is about fifteen thousand strong and is commanded by General Joseph R. Anderson. It extended several miles, and whenever we would get into a long straight piece of road where I could look back the sight was most amazing. The compact mass moved four deep, and, with their glittering guns, looked like a river of human beings.

I stood the march finely, and your brother Edwin did not seem to be jaded at all, neither did Billie. Coppock was too sick to move, so we left him behind; but I do not believe he will fall into the hands of the enemy. They are not advancing in that direction. We have been living on crackers and bacon, but I got a fine breakfast this morning on the road. General Gregg and his staff were present and I had the honor of being introduced to them all.

There is little doubt but that we shall get into a fight very soon, possibly before you receive this letter. There must be fighting somewhere on the line now, for I hear the booming of field pieces. We are well prepared for them, and whether we whip them or not they cannot whip us badly.

Take good care of yourself and George.

Henrico County, Va.
June 3, 1862
Battle of Ellyson's Mills

Our army whipped the Yankees so badly on Saturday and
Sunday (May 28-29) that there was no fighting yesterday.
I believe, though, that another fight is going on to-day, for I
hear considerable cannonading, and I saw a balloon up a
short while ago.

On Sunday I was sent to Richmond to look after our sick
and did not return until late yesterday afternoon. While there
I had an opportunity to observe the shocking results of a battle, but, instead of increasing my horror of a battlefield, it
made me more anxious than ever to be in a conflict and share
its honors. To me every wounded man seemed covered with
glory.

Our casualties were certainly very great, for every house
which could be had was being filled with the wounded. Even
the depots were being filled with them and they came pouring
into the hospitals by wagon loads. Nearly all were covered
with mud, as they had fought in a swamp most of the time
and lay out all night after being wounded. Many of them were
but slightly wounded, many others severely, large numbers
mortally, and some would die on the road from the battlefield.
In every direction the slightly wounded were seen with their
arms in slings, their heads tied up, or limping about. One man
appeared as if he had been entirely immersed in blood, yet he
could walk. Those in the hospitals had received severe flesh
wounds or had bones broken, or some vital part penetrated.
They did not seem to suffer much and but a few ever groaned,
but they will suffer when the reaction takes place. I saw one
little fellow whose thigh was broken. He was a mere child, but
was very cheerful.

Our brigade will move about four miles from here this
evening. We occupy the extreme left of Johnson's army and
may remain near here for some time, but we cannot tell.
Movements of war are very, very uncertain.

Camp near Richmond, Va.
June 26, 1862

I returned to camp on Monday because we expected to have a
fight. Our brigade was ordered away last night with two days'
rations, but I am left behind with the sick. There are a great
many sick men in the hospitals and they are dying by the
thousands. Our regiment has lost about one hundred men
since we came to Virginia.

The enemy threw shells all about our camp yesterday and
killed two horses, but only one man. It was a great day
between our batteries and those of the enemy. They fired all
day long, but as it was all at long taw little damage was done.
I went out this morning to view the enemy, and could see
them and their breastworks very distinctly.

Since I began writing this letter I hear a terrific cannonading
on the left wing of our army, and I believe the battle has
opened. I am informed that General Jackson is about there
and that a fight will certainly take place this week.

You must be cheerful and take things easy, because I believe
the war will soon be ended.

Camp near Richmond, Va.
June 29, 1862
Seven Days' Fight Around Richmond

I was correct in my last letter to you when I predicted that the
great battle had commenced (Chickahominy or Gaines Mills).
The conflict raged with great fury after I finished writing, and
it lasted from three o'clock until ten that night. The cannonading was so continuous at one time that I could scarcely hear
the musketry at all. There was one incessant boom and roar
for three hours without any cessation. Next morning (28th)
the battle began anew, but there was not nearly so much cannonading, because our men rushed upon the Yankees and
took their cannon. The musketry, though, was terrific. It

reminded me of myriads of hailstones falling upon a house
top. I could see the smoke and the bombs burst in the air, and
could hear the shouts of our men as they would capture the
Yankee batteries.

Our brigade took the advance in the morning when the battle commenced, and after we routed them we did not get a
chance to fight them again until we had driven them about
eight or ten miles from where we started them. They rallied
there and made a stand, but our troops rushed at them again
and drove them to—God only knows where! A Yankee officer
(a prisoner) told me that they had no idea General Jackson
was anywhere about here, and he acknowledged that General
McClellan was completely outwitted. I tell you the Yankee
"Napoleon" has been badly defeated.

Our Colonel surprised his men by his bravery. My brother
Billie is greatly mortified because he was too sick to be in the
fight. He is still hardly able to walk. Our regiment had eight
killed and forty wounded. Orr's Regiment and the First South
Carolina were badly cut up in an attempt to capture a battery.
(The former had 81 killed and 234 wounded, and the latter
20 killed and 125 wounded.)

I was on the ground yesterday (Saturday) where some of
the hardest fighting took place. The dead were lying everywhere and were very thick in some places. One of our
regiments had camped in some woods there and the men
were lying among the dead Yankees and seemed uncon-
cerned.

The most saddening sight was the wounded at the hospitals, which were in various places on the battlefield. Not
only are the houses full, but even the yards are covered with
them. There are so many that most of them are much neglected.
The people of Richmond are hauling them away as fast as
possible. At one place I saw the Yankee wounded and their
own surgeons attending to them. There are no crops or fences
anywhere, and I saw nothing which had escaped the Yankees
except one little Guinea fowl. I thought our army was bad

enough, but the country over which the Yankees have been looks like some barren waste. On my way to the battlefield I met a negro who recognized me and told me that your brother Edwin was wounded in the breast and had gone to Richmond. I fear there is some truth in it.

Near Orange Court House, Va.
August 12, 1862

While we are resting a little I will endeavor to write you a few lines. We have been moving about continuously since I wrote to you on the 8th inst., and have had some hard times, I assure you. Most of our hard marching has been during the night, but much of it has been in the heat of the day. We have had nothing to eat but crackers and bacon, and not nearly enough of that.

We first (on the 9th inst.) marched up into Culpeper County, and were within two miles of the battlefield (of Cedar Mountain). It was a brilliant victory for us, as two of their dead to one of ours were left on the field. On the way we met a great many prisoners, who were lively and jocose and seemed glad they were taken.

The weather has been fine, although very hot. We had one hard shower of rain, and everybody stood and took it, as there was nothing else we could do. Tell your brother he should be glad he was wounded, for it has saved him many great hardships. I never murmur at these trials, though, as long as I can have good health.

Last night we began falling back. I suppose it was some strategic move and that we will continue these active operations until a decisive fight takes place. General Jackson will not be outgeneraled, and I believe he is sure to defeat Pope. I saw him (Jackson) this morning. He is a very ordinary looking man.

I would like to write you a longer letter, but have not the

time. We are now drawing rations, and as soon as we get our meat boiled will start again. I must close, as preparations are being made to leave, so good-by for this time.

Orange County, Va.
August 18, 1862

On leaving our last camp we first went back five miles in a northerly direction to Orange Court House, and we thought Jackson intended to take us over the same road we had fallen back on a few days before; but from there we took the road to Fredericksburg. That was a mistake also, for after going about ten miles we turned to the left and went three miles toward the Rapidan River, and have stopped at this place. It is believed that Jackson intended to cross the river and flank Pope, and that the Yankees got wind of it. They were on a mountain and may have seen our large force moving. Jackson is a General who is full of resources, and if he fails in one plan he will try another.

The men stood the march better than at any previous time. The health of the brigade has improved since we are where we can breathe the pure mountain air. This beautiful country, with its mountains and rolling hills, is enough to make any sick man feel better. We all sleep out in the open air—officers as well as privates—although the weather is becoming quite cool and signs of autumn begin to appear. The crops of corn are magnificent and are almost matured, but wherever our army goes, roasting ears and green apples suffer. I have often read of how armies are disposed to pillage and plunder, but could never conceive of it before. Whenever we stop for twenty-four hours every corn field and orchard within two or three miles is completely stripped. The troops not only rob the fields, but they go to the houses and insist on being fed, until they eat up everything about the man's premises which can be eaten. Most of them pay for what they get at the houses, and are charged exorbitant prices, but a hungry soldier will give all he has for something to eat, and will then steal when hunger again harasses him. When in health and tormented by hunger he thinks of little else besides home and something to eat. He does not seem to dread the fatiguing marches and arduous duties.

A wounded soldier who has been in Jackson's army for a long time told me his men had but one suit of clothes each, and whenever a suit became very dirty the man would pull it off and wash it, and then wait until it dried. I believe this to be a fact, because when I see Jackson's old troop on the march none have any load to carry except a blanket, and many do not even have a blanket; but they always appear to be in fine spirits and as healthy and clean as any of our men. The force we have here now is a mammoth one. I am told that Lee and Johnson are both here, and I am anxious for our army to engage Pope. Whenever we start on a march I am impatient to go on and fight it out, for we are confident we can whip the enemy.

We are now cooking up two days' rations and are ordered to have them in our haversacks and be ready to move at sundown, but we may not go at that time, because sometimes we receive such orders and then do not leave for a day or two. I will write again whenever I have a chance.

Culpeper County, Va.
August 24, 1862

Our army pursued Pope's to this place last week. We are now on the west side of North Fork of the Rappahannock River, while Pope is on the other side. Each army is trying to get the advantage of the other, and it is difficult for either to cross the river while the other opposes it. It is evident that we shall have a tremendous fight in a few days. General Lee is here with us, for I saw him pass by. We have just cooked up two days' rations and are expecting every minute to leave here.

I saw a pretty little fight a few days ago when I was far in the rear with the ambulance train, and it was by the merest chance that the train was not cut off from the main force and captured. General Hood with his staff was reconnoitering, and was fired upon by the Yankees, who were under cover of some woods a little distance from the road. A Texas brigade happened to be passing and was sent against them, and whipped them badly.

There has been quite an amount of rain recently, but we have no tents, not even anything in the shape of tents.

I have a chance to send this to Gordonsville, and as the bearer is about to leave I must close. I could write you a long letter if I had time, so good-by for now.

Ox Hill, Va.
September 3, 1862

I was in the battle at Manassas and made several very narrow escapes. I had to go on the field there, although it was Dr. Kilgore's place to go, and not mine, but he was afraid to go. On Monday (September 1) at this place I came very near being killed; for a bombshell barely did miss me and burst right at me. I stood the late terrible march surprisingly well, but I have learned what hunger and hardships are. I would often lie down at night on the bare ground without a blanket or anything else to cover with and would wonder what my dear wife would think if she could see me lying there. We have had some dreadful sufferings, especially on these forced marches. The fatigue and the pangs of hunger were fearful.

We marched fast all day Monday and all day Tuesday (August 25 and 26) and until late Tuesday night, when we bivouacked in a field of tall grass near Bristow Station. Bob Land spread his wet horse blanket on a bare spot, and we lay

on it and covered with his blanket and went to sleep without
supper. The country was a waste, and I heard no sound of
a chicken, cow or dog during the night.

The next morning (Wednesday) we got up before day and
marched fast to Manassas Junction, and almost kept up with
the cavalry. We found sutlers' stores and trainloads of flour
and meat, and we captured a few prisoners. I went into a sut-
ler's tent and got three days' rations of ham, crackers and salt.
Before noon we started towards Washington, and after marching three or four miles we marched back to Manassas Junction
again late that afternoon and found many prisoners and
negroes there, who were all sent away towards Groveton. We
staid there that night, and all the cars and everything were set
on fire about the same time. We were very tired, and all day
lay down on the ground, but I remained awake for some time
watching the fire, which burned fiercely. Thursday morning
(28th) we marched nearly to Centreville, and from there
towards Groveton, and Ewell's command got into a fight late
that afternoon on our right. We remained there and
bivouacked in the oak forest where our brigade fought next
day.

Next morning (Friday) we had breakfast, and I ate with
Adjutant Goggans. Our command then took position in the
woods near the cut of an unfinished railroad and sent out
skirmishers, who soon retreated and fell back on the main
line. The Yankee line came up quite near and fired into us
from our right, and Goggans was shot through the body. I
remained some distance in rear of our line and saw Mike
Bowers, Dave Suber and two other men bringing someone
back on a litter, and I said: "Mike, who is that?" and he said:
"Goggans," just as they tumbled him down. I looked at him
as he was gasping his last, and he died at once. Then the
wounded who could walk began to come back, and those
who could not were brought to me on litters. I did all I could
for them until the ambulances could carry them to the field
infirmary, and this continued until late in the afternoon.

I saw an Irishman from South Carolina bringing a wounded
Irishman from Pennsylvania back and at the same time scold-
ing him for fighting us. Colonel McGowan came limping
back, shot through the thigh, but he refused to ride, and said:
"Take men who are worse hurt than I am." Colonel Marshall
and Lieutenant-Colonel Leadbetter were brought back mortally wounded.

Our brigade was not relieved until about four o'clock. They
had been fighting all day and their losses were very heavy.
I saw General Fields, commanding a Virginia brigade, ride in
on our left to relieve us, and I then went back to the field infirmary, where I saw large numbers of wounded lying on the
ground as thick as a drove of hogs in a lot. They were groan-
ing and crying out with pain, and those shot in the bowels
were crying for water. Jake Fellers had his arm amputated
without chloroform. I held the artery and Dr. Huot cut it off
by candle light. We continued to operate until late at night
and attended to all our wounded. I was very tired and slept
on the ground.

We did nothing Saturday morning (30th). There were several thousand prisoners near by, and I went where they were
and talked with some of them. Dr. Evans, the brigade surgeon,
went to see General Lee, and General Lee told him the battle
would begin that morning at about ten o'clock and would
cease in about two hours, which occurred exactly as he said.
Our brigade was not engaged, and we spent the day sending
the wounded to Richmond.

Early Sunday morning (31st) we started away, and I passed
by where Goggans' body lay. Near him lay the body of Captain Smith of Spartanburg. Both were greatly swollen and had
been robbed of their trousers and shoes by our own soldiers,
who were ragged and barefooted, and did it from necessity.
We passed on over the battlefield where the dead and
wounded Yankees lay. They had fallen between the lines and
had remained there without attention since Friday. We
marched all day on the road northward and traveled about
twelve miles.

The next morning (September 1) we continued our march towards Fairfax Court House, and had a battle all that afternoon at Ox Hill during a violent thunderstorm. Shell were thrown at us and one struck in the road and burst within three or four feet of me. Several burst near Colonel Edwards as he rode along, but he did not pay the slightest attention to them. There were flashes and keen cracks of lightning near by and hard showers of rain fell. The Yankees had a strong position on a hill on the right side of the road, but our men left the road and I could see them hurrying up the hill with skirmishers in advance of the line.

I went into a horse lot and established a field infirmary, and saw an old lady and her daughter fleeing from a cottage and crossing the lot in the rain. The old lady could not keep up and the daughter kept stopping and urging her mother to hurry. The bullets were striking all about the yard of their house.

Lieutenant Leopard from Lexington was brought back to me with both of his legs torn off below the knees by a shell, and another man with part of his arm torn off, but neither Dr. Kenedy, Dr. Kilgore nor our medical wagon was with us, and I had nothing with me to give them but morphine. They both died during night. The battle continued till night came on and stopped it. We filled the carriage house, barn and stable with our wounded, but I could do but little for them. Colonel Edwards was furious, and told me to tell the other doctors "for God's sake to keep with their command."

After doing all I could for the wounded, my brother, my servant Wilson, and myself went into the orchard and took pine poles from a fence and spread them on the wet ground to sleep on. I discovered a small chicken roosting in a peach tree and caught it, and Wilson skinned it and broiled it, and it was all we three had to eat that day. Wilson got two good blankets off the battlefield with "U.S." on them, and we spread one on the poles and covered with the other.

The next morning the Yankees were gone. Their General,

Kearney, was killed and some of their wounded fell into our hands. The two other doctors with our medical supplies did not get there until morning, and many of our wounded died during the night. I found one helpless man lying under a blanket between two men who were dead.

We drew two days' rations of crackers and bacon about ten o'clock, and I ate them all and was still very hungry. I walked over on the hill and saw a few dead Yankees. They had become stiff, and one was lying on his back with an arm held up. I picked up a good musket and carried it back with me to the house and gave it to the young lady I saw running away the day before. She thanked me for it, and seemed very much pleased to have it as a memento of the battle.

Late that afternoon we drew rations again, and I ate everything without satisfying my hunger. A solder came from another command and said he heard I had some salt, and he offered me a shoulder of fresh pork for some. Wilson cooked it and I ate it without crackers, but was still hungry. During the night I became very sick from overeating, and next morning when the regiment left I was too sick to march. Billie, Mose Cappock, Billy Caldwell and myself all got sick from the same cause. We are all sleeping in the carriage house, and I have sent Wilson out into the country to get something for us to eat.

We hope to be able to go on and catch up with the regiment in a day or two. It has gone in the direction of Harper's Ferry.

This is the last letter that the doctor wrote to his wife in this series.

May 2, 1865

I reached my father's home and nobody was expecting me. I was completely exhausted, but after getting on some clean, whole clothes and sleeping in a bed once more I felt greatly refreshed. Father has given me a good horse in exchange for my little mule, and I hope to be rested enough to leave here day after to-morrow and go through the county in a buggy for you.

Welch, Spencer Glasgow. *A Confederate Surgeon's Letters to His Wife*. New York and Washington: The Neale Publishing Company, 1911.

United States Sanitary Commission Memoirs

by John A. Lidell, A.M., M.D.

JOHN A. LIDELL was in charge of the Stanton U.S. Army General Hospital, where he began to collect personal observations, clinical histories, and postmortem records, a few of which are set forth in the following pages. The histories set forth occurred in the author's practice, were furnished by his professional friends, or were placed in his hands by the U.S. Sanitary Commission as contributions received by them to the surgical history of the war.

These memoirs were written in 1867, and a considerable period of time—almost four years—elapsed before their publication. The book from which they are drawn, U.S. Sanitary Commission Memoirs, is essentially clinical in character. Most of the cases were never published before 1870, but a select few appeared in medical journals.

Clinical reports on patients have undergone little change in form or style through the years. Anyone with hospital-patient experience will note that his or her doctor's account resembled in form the cold report the surgeons issued during and after the Civil War.

The author writes in his preface:

> If this book shall add anything to the domain of human knowledge, if it shall serve to account for any of the untoward results of surgical operations which before seemed strange and unaccounted for, and especially if it shall enable us to obviate any of these untoward results, then it has not been written in vain.

As we sit and look back over almost 150 years of medical advances since the Civil War, we cannot help but empathize with the human suffering and with the medical community in its search for effective treatment. We can only marvel at the rate of survival of the ill and the wounded in the nineteenth century.

CASE XXI. *Axillary Artery wounded by Rifle-ball (conical);*
Hemorrhage ceased spontaneously; Recovery without suppuration;
reported by Dr. James M. Holloway in the "American Journal
of Medical Sciences," October 1865, pp. 352, 353.

Claude H. Dinkins, corporal Light Artillery, aged 31 years,
merchant, health good, wounded July 18, 1864 near Petersburg, by a sharp-shooter. Gunshot wound (small minie ball,
which, after striking him, wounded his companion) through
the left shoulder; ball entering behind on a line with and
about two inches to the right of the axillary crease, made its
exit in front about one inch above the anterior angle of the
axilla. A note from Dr. W. M. Nash, who saw the patient in
camp a short time after receipt of wound, is as follows: "The
axillary nerves are seriously injured, and indeed the artery
does not seem to have escaped, though no hemorrhage has
occurred; the impulse in the radial artery is very slight.
July 20th, near Petersburg."

July 23.—I saw the patient for the first time this morning; he
states that he has felt the pulse at the wrist occasionally, and
that at such times he experiences a sense of fullness, as if the
arm was filling with blood. He states also that Dr. Palmer, of
Florida, has examined him frequently since admission, and
thought he could detect pulsation at the wrist. Sensation perfect in hand and arm, excepting numbness in thumb. *The*
wounds of entrance and exit are closed by clots; no discharge; no
evidence of inflammation; complains of occasional pain in the
hand. Removed to a tent and ordered moist dressings and
rest in recumbent posture.

July 24.—Rested well under influence of morphia. *I can dis-*
cover no pulse at the wrist, nor at any point along the course of the
vessel below the seat of injury. Arm cool, pain not distressing;
wound still dry, and clots undisturbed. Dr. J. B. Gaston, of
Alabama, thinks he can discover a feeble pulse at the wrist.

July 25.—Suffering from nervous twitchings in arm and

shoulder, which he mitigates by bathing the parts in cold water; *clots dissolving; no sign of pus.*

August 4.—No change of interest has occurred since last note, the case progressing favorably; *no pulse at wrist, nor discharge of pus from the wounds, which are now closed by scab;* suffers at times with severe pain throughout the limb, or, as he describes it, "along the course of the nerves."

August 13.—Furloughed, to proceed by easy stages to his home. Has not experienced an unpleasant symptom, excepting pain in the limb. The wound has healed throughout its whole tract by McCartney's "modeling process," except at the orifice of exit, where, on the 12th, a small quantity (only a few drops) of pus formed after the scab had been removed through carelessness of the nurse. *Pulsation below the seat of injury was not felt by myself at any time during the progress of the case, though repeated examinations were made.*

In the following March I heard by letter that Mr. Dinkins was enjoying excellent health, and that the wounds were entirely healed. Strength and motion of the limb somewhat impaired. The long-continued absence of pulsation in the main branches below the seat of injury in this case, forms, in my experience, an exception to the general rule.

CASE XXIII. *Axillary Artery severed by a Gunshot Projectile; Hemorrhage not troublesome; Consecutive Gangrene of the Arm.*

Private T. H. Hudson, a prisoner of war, aged 21, was admitted to the Stanton U. S. Army General Hospital, May 18, 1864. He had received two wounds from fire-arms at Spottsylvania Court-house, Va., May 11th. One ball entered his right hip near the sacrum, and made its exit from near the right groin. The other ball penetrated the left shoulder from behind, and escaped in front a little way below the clavicle.

On admission to hospital the patient's general condition

was good, and his wounds looked well. It was observed that he had no radial pulse on left side. Simple dressings were applied to the wound, and he was allowed a nourishing diet.

May 22.—The wounds appear to be doing well, but the left arm has become much swelled and dark in color. No bronchial nor radial pulse can be detected in it.

May 28.—The gangrene of the arm is still progressing. The mortified tissues of the fore-arm are exulcerating. Prescribed tint. ferri muriat gtt. xx. every four hours, together with spts. frumenti 6 fluid oz. per diem.

June 1.—The gangrene is limited at middle of arm. The wounds look well, but still he is obviously failing. He is much emaciated, his tongue is dry, his appetite poor, and he has some diarrhoea.

He continued to sink and died June 6th of exhaustion.

Comments.—Although this patient's general condition did not seem to justify us in amputating his arm at any time subsequent to the occurrence of the gangrene, because it was so low, still, on reviewing the case now, I am inclined to think that the operation might have improved his chance of recovery somewhat, especially if it had been performed as soon as the gangrene appeared. While making our criticisms upon the treatment of this case, we should, however, bear in mind that *almost every case of secondary amputation performed in Stanton Hospital during the months of May and June 1864, proved fatal,* and it is highly probable that this fact exerted no small degree of influence for inducing us to postpone the amputation of this man's gangrenous arm.

CASE XLV. *Gunshot Fracture of Lower Jaw; the Ball passed downwards into the Neck, fracturing also the Transverse*

Processes of the Third and Fourth Cervical Vertebrae; it wounded the Internal Jugular Vein and lodged; Secondary Hemorrhage repeatedly occurred.

M. A. Rupert, private Company E. 46th Ohio Volunteers, wounded at Dallas, Ga., May 27th or May 28th, 1864; admitted into hospital May 28th. A ball entered the face about the middle of the buccinator muscle, on the right side, fractured the inferior maxilla, of that side, passed downwards into the neck, on the same side and lodging, could not be felt.

May 30.—He felt well; had a good pulse and a good appetite, but could swallow liquid food only. He continued to do well until the night of June 7th, when *some hemorrhage* from the wound occurred. On the night of June 8th, *profuse hemorrhage* from the wound took place. His pulse became feeble and his appetite poor.

June 9th.—He appeared much better; pulse full; appetite good; from this time he improved.

June 14.—He was able to walk about. (There was a purulent discharge from the wound from June 3d to June 27th.)

June 26.—Appetite good; pulse full and strong.

June 27.—He felt sick in the morning. About seven o'clock *some hemorrhage* from the wound occurred, which was arrested by compressing the common carotid artery. At nine o'clock he had a *convulsion and died.*

Post-mortem Examination.—The ball had passed into the chest, having *laid the internal jugular vein open for about four inches,* and fractured the transverse precesses of the third and fourth cervical vertebrae. The tissues of the right side of the neck were infiltrated with pus.

CASE LIII. *Intermediary hemorrhage, Parenchymatous in Character, following Secondary Amputation of Thigh.* **George R. Maxwell, Lieut.-Colonel 1st Mich. Cav.; age 22. Wounded at Five Forks, Va., by conical ball, April 1st, 1865.**

The ball entered opposite head of fibula, opening the left knee-joint.

When admitted he was very anaemic; extensive suppuration had taken place; the pus was infiltrated between the muscles as high as the apex of Scarpa's triangle.

The joint was filled with pus, and the leg had become infiltrated with serum. His general condition was very unfavorable; gave him champagne and beef-tea every hour.

April 17.—No change in his condition. D. W. Bliss, Surgeon U. S. Vols., after the patient had been placed under the influence of ether, amputated the thigh by the circular operation, at middle third of femur.

The knee-joint was then found to be filled with pus, and the muscles had been separated by extensive abscesses, which extended to Scarpa's triangle.

The stump was dressed with cold water, and the patient was placed in bed, and took tinct. opii fluid one-half drachm sp. vini Gall. 2 fluid drachms to be followed by sul. morph. and beef ext. every two hours.

April 18.—*Although twelve ligatures had been applied, hemorrhage has continued to take place (he is apparently of a hemorrhagic diathesis); has lost altogether about eight ounces of blood. Applied liq. ferri persulph, fortis by a camel's-hair brush to the whole of the surface of the wound, which had been left open and exposed to the air for about fifteen minutes; this styptic entirely checked the sanguineous oozing.*

April 20.—The granulations have become healthy, and about two drachms of pus are discharged daily.

April 30.—The wounds have granulated well, and the stump is nearly closed.

June 23.—Removed a fragment of necrosed femur, of conical shape, and about four inches in length.

August 4.—Patient left for home—stump solid and in good condition.

CASE LIV. *Intermediary Hemorrhage from Arm-stump on the Fourth Day after Amputation, the Brachial Artery having not been properly secured by Ligature; arrested by opening stump and tying Artery again. Its Coats were healthy.*

Private John P. Fitzpatrick, Co. G. 52 N.Y. Vols., aged 37, sustained a gunshot fracture of his left humerus in the battle of Spottsylvania Court-house, Va. May 18th, 1864, in consequence of which his arm was then amputated, at the junction of its middle and superior third by the double flap method.

On the 21st he was admitted to the Stanton U.S. Army General Hospital

On the 23d, twelve hours after admission, he was attacked by profuse arterial hemorrhage. The dressings were immediately removed, the flaps opened, whereupon it was found that *the flow of blood proceeded from the brachial artery, which had not been properly secured by ligature in the first instance, or, at least, the ligature had slipped off from it.* The artery was then tied again upon the face of the stump by Asst. Surgeon Geo. A. Mursick, U. S. Vols. Its coats appeared healthy. He lost about sixteen ounces of blood.

May 27.—The Stump looked well, and the purlulent matter discharged was healthy.

May 29 and 30.—He had pyaemic chills and other symptoms of the purulent infection.

June 4.—He exhibited symptoms of pyaemic pneumonia, and died the same day.

The hemorrhage did not return after the last operation, that is, the one performed on the day following his admission to hospital.

CASE LV. *Profuse Intermediary Hemorrhage from a Gunshot*
Wound involving Face and Neck; it occurred on Fourth Day;
Ligation of Right Primitive Carotid Artery; the Hemorrhage
recurred; Ligation of Left External Carotid.

Dr. M. Mahon, Surgeon Ohio Vols., relates the case which
occurred in the person of a soldier, aged 25, wounded at the
storming of Mission Ridge, Nov. 25. Ball entered anterior to
left angle of lower jaw, fracturing that bone, making a ragged
opening nearly one inch long, passed downwards, and to the
right under the tongue, cutting the floor of the mouth, and
escaped from the side of the neck to the right and a little
below the great corner of the hyoid bone.

November 29.—Evening. Dr. M. was hastily called to this
patient on account of hemorrhage. The distance to the patient
was about one square. Dr. M. found him bleeding from the
right side, the blood rushing from his mouth and aperture
where the ball escaped from his neck, in a continuous stream,
which was bright arterial, and came, as was supposed from
the sublingual artery. He had already lost between three and
four pints of blood (estimated).

It was at once decided to ligate the common carotid of the
right side. The patient was placed in a semi-recumbent position, his back well supported by a nurse. It was utterly impossible for him to lie down; as it was, the blood flowed into his
mouth with such rapidity as almost to cause strangulation.
The administration of chloroform could not be entertained.
The vessel was tied just above the omo-hyoid muscle. All
hemorrhage immediately ceased. The time consumed was
extremely short, as the operation, in order to be successful,
had to be expeditiously performed. During the operation an
assistant had to introduce his finger into the patient's mouth
to free it from the clots of blood which interfered with respi-
ration. In tightening the ligature, Dr. M. watched the patient's
face to see if any effect would be produced but none was
visible except an expression of relief from the pain incidental
to the operation. He was placed upon supporting treatment
(nutrients and stimulants).

November 30.—No return of hemorrhage; had rested tolerably well; very much prostrated; pulse rapid and weak.

December 1.—Slight hemorrhage occurred from wounds on left side during night, controlled by liquor ferri persulphatis.

December 2.—Hemorrhage recurred both morning and evening.

December 3.—Last night about 12 M., hemorrhage occurred again with considerable force, which necessitated the ligation of the left external carotid. Afterwards the hemorrhage did not return.

December 4.—Patient very weak; pulse one hundred, small and feeble; appetite poor, cannot partake of solid food; has to subsist on liquids, beef-tea, farina, thin gruel, coffee, tea, and whiskey-toddy. Milk-punch he cannot bear.

December 6.—General condition somewhat improved, but he cannot sit up in bed without causing a feeling of faintness and dizziness. Pulsation can be felt on supra-orbital ridge of left side, but more distinctly on the right side. Face blanched.

December 9.—Doing well; pulse ninety, tolerable strong, with considerable volume; appetite good. Expresses himself as doing well.

From this time he continued to improve. The ligature from the external carotid separated December 11; that from the primitive, the following day.

January 28, 1864.—This man left Chattanooga on furlough for his home in Indiana, to all appearance as well as ever, except the inconvenience of being unable to masticate his food.[1]

---

[1] (Original author's note) Vide *American Journal of Medical Sciences,* (July 1864), 276–78.

CASE LVI. *Intermediary Hemorrhage from Deep Palmar Arch following Gunshot Wound of Hand; it began on the second day; Ligation of Brachial Artery; more than Four Months afterwards the Hand was attached with Sloughing; then Profuse Secondary Hemorrhage occurred; it was controlled by Styptics and Pressure;* reported by Dr. James M. Holloway.

—Isaac Herring, private 53d Regiment, Co. C.; occupation farmer; aged 24 years; general health good; wounded at the battle of Missionary Ridge, November 25, 1863. Gunshot wound (minie) of left hand; ball entering palmar aspect between first and second metacarpal bones, near their carpal extremities, and lodging under the skin on the dorsum near the ulnar side of the metacarpo-phalangeal articulation of the thumb. The ball was extracted shortly after receipt of injury. He was sent to the rear by rail on the 28th, arriving at the hospital on the evening of the 29th. His wound commenced to bleed on the morning of the 27th at the field infirmary, and continued to bleed at intervals throughout the trip; and upon arrival at the hospital was nearly pulseless.

Diagnosis.—Intermediary hemorrhage from the deep palmar arch.

November 29.—*The brachial artery was ligated in its middle third* by Dr. H., and the wound in the hand was cleansed and carefully dressed. *The pulse at the wrist was felt beating full and strong eight hours afterwards.* Extensive inflammation of the whole hand followed, and was treated with cold applications. *The hemorrhage did not recur.* He was transferred to another post forty miles distant, January 26, 1864. At that the hand and fore-arm were still somewhat inflamed; pain severe; a deep-seated palmar abscess formed, and was opened; the wrist-joint had become anchylosed. He suffered from a mild attack of erysipelas, extending up the arm and over the face.

April 9.—Being possessed of a powerful constitution, he has been able to endure an unreasonable amount of suffering, and, at present, he is walking about his ward. The cicatrices in the hand have recently commenced to ulcerate, destroying the web between the index finger and thumb. His appetite is good. It may be remarked that the pain in the hand has been at times so severe as to resist all means employed for its mitigation, even the endermic application of large doses of morphia.

April 16.—The ulceration continues; a red line extends along the flexor aspect of the arm; hand oedematous; not painful under pressure; ordered charcoal and cinchona poultice with a view to its cleansing and stimulant effect. Tension and long-standing inflammation of the tissues have destroyed their vitality.

April 20.—Ulceration has given place to sloughing, with constitutional disturbance. Surrounding tissues red, swollen, and sensitive. *Slight arterial hemorrhage occurred this morning.* Countenance anxious, and pulse irritable. Ordered nitric acid to wound, and large doses of tinct. ferri chlorid. and chlorate potassa.

April 21.—Neglected to take iron and potassa yesterday; *another slight hemorrhage this morning;* cleaned wound of slough and clots, and *dressed with charpis steeped in turpentine;* it seems disposed to take on healthy action.

April 24.—*Hemorrhage recurred this morning at daylight, and was profuse;* again at 10 A.M. The slough has extended over the thumb, and invaded the metacarpo-phalangeal articulation. *Cleaned the wound and filled it with persulphate of iron in powder. Applied a light retentive bandage, and elevated the hand.* Ordered opium gr. i., to be repeated as often as necessary to secure rest.

April 29.—Healthy action has returned and the wound is granulating. The persulphate of iron has formed a firm plug, and is being gradually loosened and pushed out.

May 1.—No more hemorrhage; wounds in good condition, and general health improving.[2]

CASE LXIV. *Gunshot Wound of Right leg (calf) in Upper Third; Secondary Hemorrhage on Forty-first Day; Ligation of Femoral Artery.*

Sergeant James Ferguson, Co. G. 142d Penn. Vols., a young man of good constitution, was admitted to Stanton U.S. Army General Hospital, December 29th, 1862, sixteen days after the first battle of Fredericksburg, on account of a gunshot wound of the right leg, received in that battle, December 13th.

The bullet passed through the calf of said leg, in its upper third, behind the tibia and fibula, in a downward and outward direction. The wound did well until the middle of January, when the granulations assumed an unhealthy appearance and the discharge became thin and serous. He also exhibited typhoid symptoms, having a hot skin, a frequent pulse, a dry, red tongue, watchfulness and no appetite. In this way he went on from January 15th until Friday morning, January 23, when hemorrhage unexpectedly occurred from the external orifice behind fibula. The officer of the day, Dr. Osborne, readily controlled the bleeding by the application of pressure with a roller bandage and ice. Dr. Osborne thought the patient lost in all about ten ounces of blood. Through that day and night the loss of blood by oozing was very little. On Saturday morning, January 24th, the bleeding recurred, from the internal orifice behind the tibia this time. Dr. Mursick, his attending surgeon, was in the ward when the bleeding commenced. He readily controlled the bleeding by the application of persulphate of iron, lint, ice, and bandaging. He lost this time from four to six ounces (not more than the last figure), of blood. In the mean time the typhoid symptoms became more marked; he complained of great tenderness throughout the leg and thigh, the inguinal glands were somewhat swollen and tender; and there was dusky redness with soreness in the track of the long

---

[2] (Original author's note) Vide *American Journal of Medical Sciences*, (Oct. 1865), 341–42.

saphenous vein. His skin was now pale yellow, and he presented other symptoms of pyaemia.

On Sunday morning a slight bleeding occurred from the internal wound, which was readily controlled by pressure and ice; there was a marked increase of swelling of the leg noticed this morning, and infiltration thereof with blood was suspected. The swelling was extending from the leg to the thigh, especially over the external and internal condyles, and the popliteal space also was already filled up with the swelling. He was very pale and sallow, and expressed a great deal of anxiety; pulse 120, quick and weak.

On Friday we thought the hemorrhage came from the peroneal artery, on Saturday from the posterior tibial; at all events, we were uncertain on Sunday morning with regard to the source of the bleeding. The case now presented an exceedingly unpromising appearance, on account of the debility from a loss of about eighteen ounces of blood, in all, not more than that, supperadded to typhoid disease condition.

It was decided to tie the femoral artery at the apex of Scarpa's space, as affording the best chance of prolonging life. That operation was accordingly performed, on the afternoon of that day, Sunday, January 25th, 1863, forty-three days after he had been wounded the patient was manifestly pyaemic, and we scarcely hoped for his recovery on that account.

Monday morning, January 26.—Patient appeared brighter, pulse 130; tongue more moist, leg getting warm, down to the ankle; plugs removed from wounds, and some dark, offensive blood flowed away. Six P.M., foot cold; leg cooler, blackness extending across the leg in track of wound; tongue dry, has had a slight chill, and he is somewhat delirious; pulse 130, and weak.

Tuesday, January 27.—Morning. Patient looks better than last evening; pulse 132, and stronger; leg warmer and blacker; foot pale and swelled (serous infiltration); serous infiltration and discoloration extends up the thigh.

Wednesday, January 28.—Patient presents a pale, yellow hue; blackness of limb deepening and extending; has reached the lower end of the incision for tying femoral artery; odor gangrenous.

Thursday, January 29.—Patient sinking; and he died in the evening, four days subsequent to the deligation of the femoral artery.

The *autopsy* showed that the bleeding came, not from the posterior tibial, nor the peroneal artery, as had been supposed, but from the lower part of the popliteal artery, which had been opened to large extent by ulceration. It was also found that the ball had grazed the hind part of both the tibia and fibula in its track, and there were some loose splinters, small in size, in relation with the tibia and fibula.

CASE LXXXVIII. *Gangrene of Stump produced by compressing it with a Tight Bandage.*

—April 10, 1865, a Confederate soldier, a prisoner of war, was brought in from the front to Burke's Railroad Junction, which was the depot of our army at the time of, and for a while after, General Lee's surrender. He had sustained amputation of the left leg at its middle, by the flap method, for gunshot injuries, and complained bitterly of pain in the stump. On removing the dressings, the bandages were found to be *very tight*, the parts compressed by them were swelled and gangrenous, and the swelling also extended above the knee.

The next morning, April 11, my attention was called to him by the surgeon in whose care he had been placed on arrival,— Dr. Snell, of the Confederate army. The patient was in a very bad condition. The stump was much swelled and very painful. The swelling extended not only as high as the knee, but also some distance up the thigh. The flaps were sphacelated, and the skin presented a yellowish-brown and mottled appearance nearly up to the knee, with several large blebs, containing a dirty, yellowish-colored serum, scattered here and there on this surface. The mortification extended as high as the strangulating bandage had been applied, but no line of separation was yet established. The odor of gangrene was strong. He complained much of pain in the mortifying part. He also had a good deal of constitutional disturbance in the shape of irritative fever. But little change, either general or local, had taken place since the previous day. He informed us that his leg was amputated on the 7th, at the front, where he was wounded; that the stump was bandaged very tightly at the first dressing, so that it gave him much distress from the outset; that the stump could not be dressed again until he reached Burke's Junction on the 10th, only three days afterwards, when the gangrenous condition above described was discovered. I directed him to be removed to the ninth Army Corps Field Hospital, which was then located in the neighborhood, as he would not bear transportation to the Depot Field Hospital at City Point.

April 14.—He is much worse, and very low; countenance almost hippocratic; the gangrene has extended up inner side of thigh almost to groin; odor of gangrene very strong; tongue dry; had been treated with tinct iodine applied locally, and opiates, stimulants, and nutrients, administered internally.

April 15.—Says he feels better, and is now free from pain; but he is in reality worse, for the mortification has continued to spread, and he is growing weaker.

April 16.—He died at four o'clock A.M. Towards the last he became delirious.

I did not meet with any other gangrenous stump among the wounded, about 2,000 in number, who were brought to Burke's Junction. The mortification could not, with propriety, be attributed to any cause besides the undue compression of the stump, which resulted from tight bandaging, aggravated by inflammatory swelling.

CASE XLV. *Gunshot Fractures of Left Femur and also of Cranium; Necrosis and Exfoliation of a Fragment of External table of skull; Chronic Osteomyelitis of Femur; Several*

Fragments of Necrosed Bone; besides some Detached Splinters,
extracted from Thigh.

Sergeant John Peters, Co. I, 115th Pennsylvania Vols., aged
25 years, was admitted to the Stanton U.S. Army General Hospital on the 15th of June, 1863, for gunshot injuries. He stated
that he was wounded on the 3d day of May in the battle of
Chancellorsville by a minie ball, which passed through his left
thigh in a backward and outward direction, and caused a
compound comminuted fracture of the femur in its middle
third. When admitted to the hospital, six weeks after the
reception of the injuries, the limb was on a double inclined
plane, the ends of the bone overlapped each other some two
or three inches, the thigh was swollen and inflamed, and the
wound suppurating profusely. There was also a large excoria-
tion in the popliteal region, caused by the pressure of the
splint.

He had besides a compound comminuted fracture of the
skull, located in the superior part of the frontal bone near the
colonal suture, and on the right side of the median line. The
scalp-wound was about two inches in length and one in
breadth. The depressed portion of the bone was about the size
of a half-dime. All the bone lying at the bottom of the scalp-
wound was denuded of the pericranium. The scalp-wound
now is rather dry, and secretes but little pus. He states that his
left side was paralyzed for about two weeks after the reception of the wound. He can move his left arm freely now, but
no opinion can be formed with regard to the paralysis of his
lower extremity, because the left thigh is fractured. He complains of having some frontal headache, and pain shooting in
the direction of his right eye. He has no other head symptoms.
His general condition is not promising. His tongue is red and
dry, his pulse frequent and feeble, his spirits are somewhat
depressed, and he has but little appetite. Treatment: the limb
was placed in Hodgen's splint, the water dressing applied to
the wounds of both the thigh and the head, and porter with a
generous diet allowed.

June 17.—He had a chill, followed by a fever and sweating. Prescribed quiniae sulph. grs. x. in solution.

June 20.—His general appearance has improved. The head-wound looks well. The denuded bone is bathed in healthy pus. The thigh wounds are also doing well.

June 25.—The wound of the head has ceased to suppurate, and the bone lying at its base is dry and white. He also has slight headache and some fever. Prescribed quiniae sulph. grs. v., acid. sulphuric. aromat. gtts. x., to be taken three times a day.

June 27.—The wound of the head is again suppurating, and he has no fever. Removed from the thigh a detached fracture-splinter about one inch in length.

July 1.—The discharge of pus from the wounds in the thigh is profuse. He looks pale and anaemic. Prescribed tinct. ferri muriat. gtts. xx., to be taken three times a day.

July 12.—He complains of having pain in the foot, which prevents sleep. Directed morphiae sulph. gr. ½ to be administered at night.

July 18.—He has diarrhoea. Prescribed pil. opiiopii (gr. i.) et camphorae (gr. ii.) to be taken every three hours.

July 25.—He has loose stools occasionally, which are controlled by the use of opium.

July 28.—Removed another detached fracture-splinter from the thigh.

August 10.—His general condition is much improved. The head-wound looks well. The fracture of the femur has united; but necrosed bone is discernible on exploration of the thigh-wound.

August 30, 31, and September 2.—He had rigors and fever in the afternoon. He took quiniae sulph. grs. x. three times a day.

September 5.—He complains of pain in his right side, is restless, has cough, and there is coarse crepitation in his right lung. The pus discharged from the thigh-wounds is profuse and fetid. He is very feeble. Ordered a jacket poultice to be applied to his chest, an expectorant mixture containing carbonate of ammonia, together with milk punch, to be taken internally, and the thigh to be dressed with liquor sodae chlorinat, dilut. as a disinfectant.

September 8.—His condition is much improved. The pain, cough, and crepitation in the chest have ceased. An exfoliation consisting of the outer laminae of the external table of the skull, three fourths of an inch in length by four tenths of an inch in breadth, was removed from the head-wound to-day. Prescribed acid. phosphoric. dilut. gtts. xx., to be taken every six hours.

September 11.—There is swelling, redness, and pain in his thigh. Ordered the lead and opium wash to be applied to it.

September 12.—The pain, redness, swelling, and tension of his thigh have increased. *Free incisions were made (long and deep), a quantity of pus evacuated, and relief afforded.*

September 14.—His general condition is much improved. The swelling and inflammation of the thigh is much diminished.

September 20.—Wound of head is healed; abscess of thigh filling up with healthy granulations.

October 1.—A small abscess has formed in the external side of the thigh; *incised it.*

November 1.—There are now three sinuses leading down through the soft parts to the femur at the place of fracture. Dead bone can be felt at the bottom; but it is not loose. His general condition is excellent.

December 20.—He complains of debility and want of appetite; is pale and anaemic, and the thigh continues to discharge freely. Prescribed extract. nucis vomicae gr. ⅙, ferri et quiniae citrat. grs. iii., to be taken three times a day.

January 18, 1864.—Extracted a large fragment of necrosed bone from the thigh through the anterior wound.

February 13.—He has diarrhoea. The evacuations are profuse and fetid. Prescribed ol. ricini f. one ounce tinct. opii, gtts. xxx dose.

February 14.—The diarrhoea continues. Ordered pil. opii (gr. i.) et camphorae (gr. i.) to be taken after each stool.

February 16.—The diarrhoea is checked. Prescribed tinct. ferri muriat. gtts. xx. to be taken three times a day as he is weak and anaemic.

February 22.—Removed a loose fragment of necrosed bone from the thigh.

March 28.—Again removed a loose fragment of necrosed bone, and through the posterior wound. The anterior wound is granulating finely. Considerable necrosed bone can still be felt through the posterior wound, but it is not loose.

April 14.—The patient was transferred to Philadelphia, Pa., being in good flesh and spirits, and abundantly able to stand the journey. The injured limb is recovering from the atrophy occasioned by long disuse, that is, it is increasing in size, and the patient is rapidly regaining the use of it.

The limb was shortened just three inches.

Lidell, John A., A.M., M.D., edited by Hamilton, Frank H. *United States Sanitary Commission Memoirs*. New York: Hurd and Houghton, 1870.

In Hospital and Camp

by Sophronia E. Bucklin

AS THE WAR *progressed, the shortage of permanent hospitals caused a rush to conversion of large buildings, warehouses, colleges, and churches to medical facilities that could house hundreds of men. The furious activity to create clinics with adjoining dormitories was noted both north and south of the Mason-Dixon line.*

A shortage of trained personnel compounded the problem, and women began to answer the nursing call, much to the chagrin of doctors and male orderlies. It was an uphill battle for the ladies of mercy to be accepted as nurses and not domestics. When Dorothea Dix[1] was appointed superintendent of women, she was in the forefront in the conflict to place responsible women in responsible positions.

Major cities soon boasted many hospitals. Washington and its suburbs had more than twenty-five general hospitals, with an excess of twenty thousand beds. One of the institutions, Judiciary Square Hospital, was the initial post for a brand-new nurse, Sophronia E. Bucklin. Her first day on the new job is described in her book, In Hospital and Camp, *published in 1869.*

---

[1] Dorothea Lynde Dix (1802–87) was an American social reformer who pioneered in the movement for specialized treatment for the insane. During the Civil War, she was appointed superintendent of women war nurses.

In the sinking of heart which fell upon me, as I saw the
great stretch of low unpainted buildings, which filled the
space at my side, it was necessary to summon all the latent
courage in my soul before I could gain courage enough to
enter. Somehow I knew I must be sustained, I should not be
forsaken for doing my plain duty, and I gave myself up to
the drifting current.

It was of my own seeking; I had been eager to lend myself
to the glorious cause of Freedom, and now, on the threshold of
the hospital in which gaping wounds, and fevered, thirsting
lips awaited me, telling their ghastly tales of the bloody battle,
my cheek flushed, and my hand grew hot and trembling.
Weak flesh and timid heart would have counseled flight, but a
strong will held them in abeyance, and the doors opened to
receive me.

I was shown to my quarters, and kindly welcomed by
Miss Clark, the woman nurse from whom I was to take my
instructions.

Urging me occupy one of the two beds which were in the
room, and remarking upon my tired worn look, she left me
with an injunction to try hard to rest, while she must hasten
away to the bedside of a dying man in our ward.

I had never been so near death before. The horror of its
nearness had never chilled my heart till now. I could not
sleep. My brain seemed on fire; the groans of suffering men
echoing on all sides, aroused me to the highest pitch of
excitement.

Was it any wonder that mortal weakness shrank from con-
fronting the hard cold realities of sharpest anguish like this?
Would you question the courage of the soldier who braved
death, charging intrepidly upon the enemy's works, if you
knew that in his heart, a moment before the blow met it, was
the wild thought, "O, why did I leave home, wife, friends
and children for this?"

The human heart is a complex thing. It may lie bare and
quivering at your feet to await the stroke, and yet give no
signs of the terror with which it awaits the transfixing blow.

Sounds of woe resounded about me, mingled now and then

with hilarious laughter. I wondered if ever in this bare room, with only the length of an unpainted board for the partition walls between wards, halls, nurses quarters, and all other officers, I should ever close my eyes to such sleep as used to come to their lids before they beheld grim-visaged war catch up the death dealing weapons.

A shuffling past my door started me to my feet, and when Miss Clark returned with the information that the man was dead, and carried to the dead-house, fancy painted the picture of the stark stiffening corpse, as careless feet walked through the hall, bearing the dead out from amidst the living.

The porter's call of, "Dinner for the ladies—turn out for dinner—all things are ready—turn in to dinner," was a welcome cry, for I had eaten nothing substantial for two days.

The dinner consisted of a leg of beef, not very well dressed, dry beans, and bread in which the grit set my teeth on edge. The Potomac water furnished our beverage, and sufficed to wash down the morsel which rebelliously stuck in our throats.

There was no duty for me that day, and after dinner was over, I went with Miss Clark to the dead-house to see the man who died in the morning.

Could I ever suppress the shuddering that passed over me, as I entered the low wooden house, in which on rude benches lay the cold white corpses of three men? Miss Clark uncovered the face of the man who died last, and told me his story—of the wife and three children in the far West, who were yet to know how it had gone with their soldier. He was wounded in the second battle of Bull Run, and had been under her care for ten days.

A cloth saturated with blood lay over a bench, and I was wrought upon by the sadness of the scene, and the echoing of many groans coming from the wards, that I only desired to hasten away from the dreadful place, and forget that it was man against his brother man, who was causing this awful destruction.

I clung to Miss Clark with the tenacity of long established friendship in these first experiences of hospital service. She was a New England woman—whole-hearted, and ready to

sacrifice her own comfort at any time, if by so doing she could
ease the pain of any sick or suffering soldier. She was a
Christian woman, sending the light of real consolation into
the darkness to cheer the dying, and lift up those on whom, in
the throes of agony, despair was preying.

And many such women, with true hearts, went down to be
the soldiers' friend, regarding privations, and sickness, and
toil as of little consequence, if some eyes over which the film
of death was stealing, could look upon them and die in
the calm belief that a mother, or wife, or sister was standing
by the bedside, smoothing the pillow, and moistening the
parched lips.

At the usual time we were called to a supper, consisting of
the same dark, dirty bread, with dried apple-sauce, and tea
which was black with strength. An introductory visit to the
wards, in which my labors were to commence so soon, ended
the long, strange day. I looked upon the narrow iron bedsteads furnished with bed of straw, one straw pillow, two
sheets, one blanket and counterpane, three rows of which ran
the length of the long room, forming narrow passage ways
through which we walked and I said to myself, "I will do this
work—not of myself have I strength, but the Lord being my
helper, I shall be enabled to do that good labor for which my
hands have been so long waiting."

The night, dragging its weary hours along—for they were
not winged by sleep—came to me with visions of battle fields
strewn with horror; sounds as of blood trickling from many
wounds; green grass and waving grain trodden by artillery;
and the woods made the hiding places of ten thousand
deaths. Lovely plains stretched out before me, on which the
harvest, just mown, was not yet prepared for flesh, and blood,
and muscle. Then the scene changed to home with its peaceful
pressures; friends greeting each other in the hazy September
mornings; work, which at the distance seemed mere pastime;
the quiet woods, the meadows ankle deep with their rich food
and the well-rounded cattle ranging over them; the blue lake
lying like a gem in the loveliest of vallies.

All these came to my pillow that night, and haunted me

with a strange restiveness which drove slumber from my eyelids.

The morning of the nineteenth of September dawned over the long low hospital, and my duties began. With silent prayers for courage, and struggling with the beating at my heart, armed with wash bowl, soap and towels, I went into the ward, and entered upon my first work as a hospital nurse, amongst those who had been wounded in fighting the second battle of Bull Run.

It was no small matter for me to apply the wet towel to the faces of bronzed and bearded men; it was no slight task to comb out the tangled hair and part it over foreheads which seemed hot with the flash of cannon. I had been nurtured in quietude, and had little conception of the actual state of things when the timid heart preferred to remain in that state, though the brain and hand were in rebellion to it, and held it down to the servitude.

I did not fancy it would wear off so soon. I did not think when, shudderingly, I first looked into the dead-house, and saw the three icy corpses, that these feet would ever stumble over stiff mortal clay, and hardly pause to note what lay within their path.

It was wonderful to me to see the universal childishness with which each threw himself upon our sympathies, and related, as to a mother, the history of the fight, the position in which he was shot, the length of time which he passed on the battle ground, the final removal, and most of all, the deep thankfulness with which he received our attention.

Women's help had not been counted upon, when, in the first tumultuous rush of excited feeling, the citizen enlisted to serve under the banner of the soldier. And when her hand with its softer touch pressed on the aching forehead, and bathed the fevered face, words failed in the attempt to express the gratitude of a full heart.

For several successive mornings one poor fellow, whose eyes were both shot out, with his head badly shattered, lay silent while his ablutions were being performed. I thought he had perhaps lost his speech in the untold terror of his sight-

less condition, but by-and-by he said, "Thank you," when the
process of washing was completed.

I could not comb his hair, for the bandages were bound
tightly over it, and, as he turned away after the simple recog-
nition of thanks, I passed on without questioning him. A few
days went by, then he said, "Did you notice that I never talked
to you, as other patients did, when you first came to take care
of us?" I replied, "I did."

"Then I will tell you why," he continued; "I was so thank-
ful, that I had no words for speech—to think the women
of the North should come down here, and do so much for us,
being exposed to all kinds of disease, and to so much work
and hard fare, all to take care of us poor soldiers, when we lie
as I do."

I inquired how he came to be a soldier, he seeming so
young, and barely of the requisite age to serve his country. He
told me the same old story of enthusiastic desire to do for his
country in her hour of peril, and it seemed a cowardly thing
to stand back, and let others share all the dangers, when he,
too, had a land to save. When those, who were reared among
the same hills, were going out to the beat of the drum to fight,
and die if God so willed it, he felt like a craven to linger behind.

While at the place of enlistment, in the very act of signing
his name, his father appeared, and forbade the act, took him
home, and confined him within the house. But the patriotism
in his boyish heart grew beyond all bounds, and he eluded
his jailor in season to go out amongst the boys, with whom he
had hunted squirrels, and roamed the woods in search of
autumn's dropping nuts, to be hoarded up for winter.

It was all over now. He had done all that he could for the
dear old flag—he had been shattered, and left a useless thing
to die among the numerous dead around him on that terrible
field. He had lain for eleven days amongst the rotting, putrid
throng—the horrors shut out, indeed, from his sight, but with
his other senses, sharpened by the sounds of pain, revealing
to his ears and imagination the real nature of the scene around
him. His only food during that time was two hard biscuits,
which he shaved down with his pocket knife, and moistened

with a few drops of water, that had remained in his canteen. Then, too, this had to be drawn into his mouth with his tongue, for he could not move his jaws.

Another soldier, wounded in the limbs, and unable to move away, made himself known to the blind man, and to avoid starvation, they agreed each to help the other, one having the eyes, and the other the limbs. Thus staggering under the weight, the exhausted soldier started from the awful spot, where death was holding high carnival. O! the soul sickens at the thought of the sights shut out to the one, but to the other only too palpable—the horrible flow of blood; the putrid masses of human flesh; the gleaming bones, from which everything had fallen clean; but over the despair—the sickness almost unto death—the love of life fluttered like a prisoned bird, and would not let them droop.

Then, like hyenas snuffing the scent of prey in the hot air, in the likeness of humanity, but void of its soul, vampires came upon the ground, rifling the bodies of the slain. To these creatures, many of the wounded turned, imploring them to convey them from that place of death, to prison, anywhere away from the horrors, which hourly grew greater and greater.

Some were taken to a rebel hospital, and their wounds were there dressed by Union soldiers, who were also held as prisoners of war. Soon after they were exchanged, and the gratitude in the soldier's heart, when he heard a woman's step about his bedside, and felt the touch of her hand upon his pillow was indeed too great for utterance.

A father came after a while to see his son, and as he looked upon the sightless eyes, he groaned in bitterness of spirit, "O, my son, if you had only obeyed your father you would have been spared this affliction. Now you can never look upon the world again, henceforth and forever darkness is over your vision!"

"But," said the patriotic boy, "the loss of my sight is nothing in comparison to the sufferings which filled my soul, when I thought how they needed me to help fight the battles for freedom, and I was held from going!"

He recovered his health, and went forth into a darkened

world; and though his eyes shall no more behold the fair land
for which he had made so terrible a sacrifice, his name is
inscribed upon the lists of Fame as one of earth's demi-gods,

ENNOBLED BY HIMSELF, BY ALL APPROVED.

Forty-six wounded men lay helpless on the iron bedsteads
in our ward at Judiciary Square Hospital, and from out the
hall enough more had gone into the convalescents' room, to
swell the entire number under our care to eighty. Each of
the fourteen wards, which projected in wings from the long
central building, held also its full quota.

Amongst the wounded were many hopelessly shattered,
who would henceforth drag useless members through life,
and some who would miss forever the good stout limbs
which lay in the trenches of Manassas.

A minnie ball had passed through both ankles of one—
another had a fractured thigh—a shot in the head destroyed
the senses of another; and one with his back bone severely
injured was compelled to lay upon his face through the
tedious hours.

Every case was different and nearly all seemed suffering to
the greatest extent of human endurance. Only that first strong
hope in life which is implanted in all our species kept up their
sinking courage, and enabled them to bear bravely the throes
of pain.

Our duties here were to distribute food to the patients,
when brought up from the kitchen; wash the faces and hands,
and comb the heads of the wounded; see that their bedding
and clothing was kept clean and whole, bring pocket handkerchiefs, prepare and give the various drinks and stimulants
at such times as they were ordered by the surgeon.

I dropped into my desired sphere at once, and my whole
soul was in the work. Every man wore the look of a hero in
my eyes, for had they not faced the red death from thundering
artillery, and braved the deadly shots of the "minnies?" Had
they not stood fearlessly, when like leaves of the autumn
before a howling blast, they had fallen thick and fast—

bronzed and dripping with gore—faces forward in the black mud of the trenches?

Home, with its joys and peaceful pleasures, was well-nigh forgotten. I remembered them all as the faint sounds of music are remembered, when the being is wholly wrapped up in new and intense thought. The horrors of the first day had faded from my vision—wounds and suffering became habitual sights, and the absorbing nature of hospital labor gradually hardened my nerves to the strength of steel.

Surgeons and officers were very kind to us, but they gave stringent orders which we were sometimes almost willing to disobey. The red tape, as the soldiers termed it, required too much official ceremony in the untying—we would rather break the string, and in serving the wounded hurriedly throw away the pieces.

Women nurses were not allowed to go into the kitchen for articles of any kind; consequently the patients were many times obliged to go without the countless little comforts which a sick fancy craves. We devised many ways to relieve their wants, begging tea, sugar, and other luxuries of loyal ladies— of Miss Dix, of State agents, and of Sanitary and Christian Commissions, and when these failed us, the boys took the hard earned pay of soldiers, and sent out for the articles themselves. We would prepare it for them by slipping a basin of water into the stove in the ward, and by dropping the tea into it when boiling.

It was then taken to our quarters, and carried thence in a bowl, having all the appearance of official ordering, if a surgeon of the officer of the day chanced to pass through the ward. The men had for their food whatever the surgeon chose to order for them while on his daily rounds. Their meals usually consisted, for the severest cases, of tea, toast, rice, milk, eggs, gruel, and chicken soup. Others generally had a tin cup two-thirds full of tea or coffee, and sugar and milk, with potatoes, meats, soups, bread and butter often for dinner.

It was Miss Dix's wish that we should learn to dress wounds, but we were peremptorily ordered from the ward, when that process was in operation. One day I was sent out with an abrupt, "Nurse, we can dispense with your services now," and, retiring to our room, I stretched myself upon my little bedstead to ease my weary feet and limbs.

While, in this position, I lay thinking of my work, a tall woman, habited in black, came in with noiseless steps, and appeared before me. She put various questions to me, with an authority which I was too startled to dispute. She gave me instructions in regard to duty, lectured me roundly on this seeming neglect, and when my lips opened to plead my defence, an admonitory, "hush," from the strange figure closed them again.

I was altogether too young for a nurse, she said. Then came visions of disgrace—of the shame which would overcome me, if Miss Dix should send me home for this grave fault, concerning which I had no conception but that of innocence. My pride rose at the thought, and when an order came, summoning me to appear before Miss Dix at seven o'clock on the following morning, I felt like the culprit, who is about to be led into court for sentence, for I had discovered, on inquiry, that my strange visitor was no other than the Superintendent of Women Nurses.

I found her busy with letters, and after watching her in uneasy nervousness, as she dashed off two or three, I gathered courage enough to say, "Miss Dix, I should like to return as soon as possible to my duties."

She replied, "You can go, dear," at the same time she opened a drawer in her table, and took therefrom a five dollar bill, which she handed me, saying, "This is not pay—only a little present from me."

I took it in confusion, and, as she bade me a kind "Good-morning," I hastened back to the hospital, feeling like the prisoner, who has unexpectedly received his acquittal, and finished the duties of the day with unwonted cheerfulness.

Mine was only a temporary assignment for instruction. Miss Clark had been there only four weeks on my arrival, and neither of us knew that our true rank was next to the surgeon of the ward. Consequently, when the head nurse imposed upon us the washing of dishes for the whole ward, although

with demurring among ourselves, and considerable questioning as to the duty, we wielded the dish cloth for days, soiling
our clothing, and often busily employed when we knew we
needed the hours for rest.

But a change soon came over the spirit of this dream,
brought about by my usual unsophisticated manner. One of
our convalescents said to me one evening, while standing in
the hall, "Miss Bucklin, there's a letter for you in the office,"
and my reply, "I wish you had brought it down," drew forth
the offer to go and fetch it. Our nurse, seeing us in conversation, roughly ordered the boy into his room, I protesting
mildly that "he was doing no hurt out of it a moment."

The man repeated his command, at the same time pushed
the boy violently through the door, and closed it. Presently
there appeared a pair of red pants, a blue jacket above, and
the whole surmounted by a red cap, with the usual tassel pen-
dant—the garb of a soldier, who, stalking out, demanded to
know what was the matter? "Why he was thus badgering the
women? he had heard enough of it; it had been going on
ever since we had been there, and now it must be ended."

He sent a blow at the nurse, which, overreaching him,
pushed me backward into the scullery, and cut off my escape,
while they struggled each to reach a knife from the shelves
their hands clenched with murderous intent. A guard was
summoned, and the zouave stated the case, while the crest-
fallen nurse hurled defiance at him from his scowling visage.

"And we both live in New York," the soldier said, "and we
may meet some day; but for fear we won't, I will give you the
rest now,"—jumping at him, and dealing heavy blows thick
and fast, the men looking on calmly till it was ended. He then
went quietly away with the guard, and the nurse was invisi-
ble for two days.

At the end of that time, after due inquiries by the proper
officials, he received his relief papers, and our dishwashing
was ended; a boy having been detailed for that purpose,
as was the regular method.

A young New York captain, named Stephens, received a
box full of tempting things from home one day, and the gener-

ous fellow could not enjoy it alone; no selfish hoarding of the dainty bits for his own palate would satisfy the whole-hearted soldier, and he gave the contents into my hands for distribution in the ward.

In my eagerness to give each one able to eat it a slice of cake, and a bit of the buttered bread, I lost all thought of its being forbidden to give such articles without the consent of the surgeon, and cutting the several loaves of cake in pieces, and nicely buttering the slices of bread from the contents of a little tin can also in the box, I went round with the loaded tray in triumph.

While in the midst of the excitement, the officer of the day came into the ward; and before I was aware of his presence, laid his hand heavily on my shoulders, saying distinctly, "Nurse, what are you doing?"

Had a thunder-bolt fallen at my feet I could not have been more startled. My heart leaped into my throat, and almost suffocated me with its throbbings. I had been doing an extraordinary thing; an act strictly forbidden by the officials of the hospital, and in my terror I expected the doom of utter disgrace and dismissal from the service.

My relief came from the captain, whose bounty I was dispensing, as he said quickly, "Doctor, the ward surgeon gave her leave to distribute these things."

"Oh, it's all right then," was the reply, and the empty tray soon was laid aside. The contents of the captain's box was a day's treat to the soldiers of the ward.

I sat one evening, after my duties were over, thinking how happy I would be to see every man in the hospital sent home, recovered in health and spirits, and wondering if death waited for any amongst them. My meditations were broken in upon by the appearance of an orderly, commanding me to report to Miss Dix without delay.

I obeyed forthwith, but instead of written instructions, verbal ones only awaited me from her housekeeper. The matter being somewhat mixed, instead of being assigned to permanent duty at Judiciary Square, and Miss Clark going to Thirteenth Street Hospital to take care of a nurse who was down with the measles, I was sent to the latter place, and the change came like a blow upon me. I had become so much interested in the welfare of each patient, had made each one's history the story of a brother, and how could I leave them, without feeling pangs of the regret, which comes not at the severing of common friendships.

I hesitated at the thought of the new faces—the new ways which I must learn—but as I was under military control, nothing remained for me but to obey without a murmur. The soldier may not choose in what ditch he will die; he may not say under whose generalship he will be led out to battle; he is only one little part of the giant machine which is to crush out wrong by its resistless might—and why was I better than our boys in blue?

Bucklin, Sophronia E. *In Hospital and Camp*. Philadelphia: John E. Potter and Company, 1869.

Hospital Sketches

by Louisa May Alcott

THE NURSING SERVICE *during the war years attracted women from all strata of society. Most of the ladies felt the urge to serve the cause in whatever capacity they could. Women who were not able to leave their homes because of familial responsibilities found many ways to help: They gathered lint for bandages, made candles, baked, and cooked food for relatives and friends who were with the troops or in hospitals. Women with freedom of movement and a strong maternal instinct gravitated to the nursing service.*

One such individual, young, bright, and headstrong, was Louisa May Alcott. At age thirty, after a hodgepodge of jobs in an attempt at carving a career, she entered the nursing service in the Union Hospital at Georgetown.

Louisa May Alcott had obtained her education almost entirely from her father, although Henry David Thoreau was an early instructor. She also received guidance from Ralph Waldo Emerson and Theodore Parker. She started writing as a young woman. At the age of sixteen, she wrote her first book, but it wasn't published until six years later. In an attempt to augment her family's income, she tried sewing, teaching, and domestic service. At age seventeen she showed a talent for acting and took her fling at the stage, but she soon fell back to writing plays rather than performing. Only one of her plays seemed to have value to a producer, who purchased the rights but never moved it into production.

Alcott found she met with more success in having her poems and short stories published after she had become a nurse. Her letters home from the hospital where she served were first published by Frank B. Sanborn in the Boston newspaper The Commonwealth *in 1863. Later that year, the collection of letters was published in an 1863 book titled* Hospital Sketches, *and it was prefaced with the following:*

> A considerable portion of this volume was published in successive numbers of *The Commonwealth*, newspaper, of Boston. The sudden popularity the Sketches won from the general public, and the praise they received from literary men of distinguished ability, are sufficient reasons,—were any needed,—for their re-publication, thus revised and

enlarged, in this more convenient and permanent form. As, besides paying the Author the usual copyright, the publisher has resolved to devote at least five cents for every copy sold to the support of orphans made fatherless or homeless by the war, no reproduction of any part of the contents now first printed in these pages will be permitted in any journal. Should the sale of the little book be large, the orphans' percentage will be doubled.

Boston, August, 1863

Louisa May Alcott rendered efficient service at the Union Hospital at Georgetown, in Washington, D.C., until her health broke down. In later years Alcott attained international fame with her novels. The foremost among them was Little Women.

"They've come! they've come! hurry up, ladies—you're wanted."

"Who have come? the rebels?"

This sudden summons in the gray dawn was somewhat startling to a three days' nurse like myself, and, as the thundering knock came at our door, I sprang up in my bed, prepared

"To gird my woman's form,
And on the ramparts die,"

if necessary; but my room-mate took it more coolly, and, as she began a rapid toilet, answered my bewildered question,—

"Bless you, no child; it's the wounded from Fredericksburg; forty ambulances are at the door, and we shall have our hands full in fifteen minutes."

"What shall we have to do?"

"Wash, dress, feed, warm and nurse them for the next three months, I dare say. Eighty beds are ready, and we were getting impatient for the men to come. Now you will begin to see hospital life in earnest, for you won't probably find time to sit down all day, and may think yourself fortunate if you get to bed by midnight. Come to me in the ball-room when you are ready; the worst cases are always carried there, and I shall need your help."

So saying, the energetic little woman twirled her hair into a button at the back of her head, in a "cleared for action" sort of style, and vanished, wrestling her way into a feminine kind of pea-jacket as she went.

I am free to confess that I had a realizing sense of the fact that my hospital bed was not a bed of roses just then, or the prospect before me one of unmingled rapture. My three days' experiences had begun with a death, and, owing to the defalcation of another nurse, a somewhat abrupt plunge into the superintendence of a ward containing forty beds, where I spent my shining hours washing faces, serving rations, giving medicine, and sitting in a very hard chair, with pneumonia on

one side, diptheria on the other, two typhoids opposite, and a
dozen dilapidated patriots, hopping, lying, and lounging
about, all staring more or less at the new "nuss," who suffered
untold agonies, but concealed them under as matronly an
aspect as a spinster could assume, and blundered through her
trying labors with a Spartan firmness, which I hope they
appreciated, but am afraid they didn't. Having a taste for
"ghastliness," had rather longed for the wounded to arrive,
for rheumatism wasn't heroic, neither was liver complaint, or
measles; even fever had lost its charms since "bathing burning
brows" had been used up in romances, real and ideal. But
when I peeped into the dusky street lined with what I at first
had innocently called market carts, now unloading their sad
freight at our door, I recalled sundry reminiscences I had
heard from nurses of longer standing, my ardor experienced a
sudden chill, and I indulged in a most unpatriotic wish that I
was safe at home again, with a quiet day before me, and no
necessity for being hustled up, as if I were a hen and had only
to hop off my roost, give my plumage a peck, and be ready for
action. A second bang at the door sent this recreant desire to
the right about, as a little woolly head popped in, and Joey, (a
six years' old contraband,) announced—

"Miss Blank is jus' wild fer ye, and says fly round right
away. They's comin' in, I tell yer, heaps on 'em—one was took
out dead, and I see him,—hi! warn't he a goner!"

With which cheerful intelligence the imp scuttled away,
singing like a blackbird, and I followed, feeling that Richard
was *not* himself again, and wouldn't be for a long time to
come.

The first thing I met was a regiment of the vilest odors that
ever assaulted the human nose, and took it by storm. Cologne,
with its seven and seventy evil savors, was a posy-bed to it;
and the worst of this affliction was, every one had assured me
that it was a chronic weakness of all hospitals, and I must bear
it. I did, armed with lavender water, with which I so besprin-
kled myself and premises, that I was soon known among
my patients as "the nurse with the bottle." Having been run

over by three excited surgeons, bumped against by migratory
coal-hods, water-pails, and small boys, nearly scalded by an
avalanche of newly-filled tea-pots, and hopelessly entangled
in a knot of colored sisters coming to wash, I progressed by
slow stages up stairs and down, till the main hall was
reached, and I paused to take breath and a survey. There they
were! "our brave boys," as the papers justly call them, for
cowards could hardly have been so riddled with shot and
shell, so torn and shattered, nor have borne suffering for
which we have no name, with an uncomplaining fortitude,
which made one glad to cherish each like a brother. In they
came, some on stretchers, some in men's arms, some feebly
staggering along propped on rude crutches, and one lay stark
and still with covered face, as a comrade gave his name to be
recorded before they carried him away to the dead house. All
was hurry and confusion; the hall was full of these wrecks
of humanity, for the most exhausted could not reach a bed till
duly ticketed and registered; the walls were lined with rows
of such as could sit, the floor covered with the more disabled,
the steps and doorways filled with helpers and lookers on; the
sound of many feet and voices made that usually quiet hour
as noisy as noon; and, in the midst of it all, the matron's motherly face brought more comfort to many a poor soul, than the
cordial draughts she administered, or the cheery words that
welcomed all, making of the hospital a home.

The sight of several stretchers, each with its legless, armless,
or desperately wounded occupant, entering my ward, admon-
ished me that I was there to work, not to wonder or weep; so I
corked up my feelings, and returned to the path of duty,
which was rather "a hard road to travel" just then. The house
had been a hotel before hospitals were needed, and many of
the doors still bore their old names; some not so inappropriate
as might be imagined, for that ward was in truth a *ball-room*, if
gun-shot wounds could christen it. Forty beds were prepared,
many already tenanted by tired men who fell down anywhere, and drowsed till the smell of food roused them. Round
the great stove was gathered the dreariest group I ever saw—

ragged, gaunt and pale, mud to the knees, with bloody bandages untouched since put on days before; many bundled up
in blankets, coats being lost or useless; and all wearing that
disheartened look which proclaimed defeat, more plainly than
any telegram of the Burnside blunder. I pitied them so much,
I dared not speak to them, though, remembering all they had
been through since the fight at Fredericksburg. I yearned to
serve the dreariest of them all. Presently, Miss Blank tore me
from my refuge behind piles of one-sleeved shirts, old socks,
bandages and lint; put basin, sponge, towels, and a block of
brown soap into my hands, with these appalling directions:

"Come my dear, begin to wash as fast as you can. Tell them
to take off socks, coats and shirts, scrub them well, put on
clean shirts, and the attendants will finish them off, and lay
them in bed."

If she had requested me to shave them all, or dance a horn-
pipe on the stove funnel, I should have been less staggered;
but to scrub some dozen lords of creation at a moment's
notice, was really—really—. However, there was no time for
nonsense, and having resolved when I came to do everything
I was bid, I drowned my scruples in my wash-bowl, clutched
my soap manfully, and, assuming a business-like air, made
a dab at the first dirty specimen I saw, bent on performing my
task *vi et armis* if necessary. I chanced to light on a withered
old Irishman, wounded in the head, which caused that portion of his frame to be tastefully laid out like a garden, the
bandages being the walks, his hair the shrubbery. He was so
overpowered by the honor of having a lady wash him, as he
expressed it, that he did nothing but roll up his eyes, and bless
me, in an irresistible style which was too much for my sense
of the ludicrous; so we laughed together, and when I knelt
down to take off his shoes, he "flopped" also, and wouldn't
hear of my touching "them dirty craters. May your bed above
be aisy darlin', for the day's work ye are doon! —Whoosh!
there ye are, and bedad, it's hard tellin' which is the dirtiest,
the fut or the shoe." It was; and if he hadn't been to the fore, I
should have gone on pulling under the impression that the

"fut" was a boot, for trousers, socks, shoes and legs were a
mass of mud. This comical tableau produced a general grin, at
which propitious beginning I took heart and scrubbed away
like any tidy parent on a Saturday night. Some of them took
the performance like sleepy children, leaning their tired heads
against me as I worked, others looked grimly scandalized,
and several of the roughest colored like bashful girls. One
wore a soiled little bag about his neck, and as I moved it, to
bathe his wounded breast, I said,

"Your talisman didn't save you, did it?"

"Well I reckon it did, marm, for that shot would a gone
a couple a inches deeper but for my old mammy's camphor
bag," answered the cheerful philosopher.

Another, with a gun-shot wound through the cheek, asked
for a looking-glass, and when I brought one, regarded his
swollen face with a dolorous expression, as he muttered—

"I vow to gosh, that's too bad! I warn't a bad looking chap
before, and now I'm done for; won't there be a thunderin'
scar? and what on earth will Josephine Skinner say?"

He looked up at me with his one eye so appealingly that I
controlled my risibles, and assured him that if Josephine
was a girl of sense, she would admire the honorable scar, as a
lasting proof that he had faced the enemy, for all women
thought a wound the best decoration a brave soldier could
wear. I hope Miss Skinner verified the good opinion I so
rashly expressed of her, but I shall never know.

The next scrubbee was a nice looking lad, with a curly
brown mane, honest blue eyes, and a merry mouth. He lay on
a bed, with one leg gone, and the right arm so shattered that it
must evidently follow: yet the little sergeant was as merry
as if his afflictions were not worth lamenting over; and when
a drop or two of salt water mingled with my suds at the sight
of this strong young body, so marred and maimed, the boy
looked up, with a brave smile, though there was a little quiver
of the lips, as he said,

"Now don't you fret yourself about me, miss; I'm first rate
here, for it's nuts to lie still on this bed, after knocking about

in those confounded ambulances, that shake what there is left
of a fellow to jelly. I never was in one of these places before,
and think this cleaning up a jolly thing for us, though I'm
afraid it isn't for you ladies."

"Is this your first battle, Sergeant?"

"No, miss; I've been in six scrimmages, and never got a
scratch till this last one: but it's done the business pretty thoroughly for me, I should say. Lord! what a scramble there'll be
for arms and legs, when we old boys come out of our graves,
on the Judgment Day; wonder if we shall get our own again?
If we do, my leg will have to tramp from Fredericksburg,
my arm from here, I suppose, and meet my body, wherever it
may be."

The fancy seemed to tickle him mightily, for he laughed
blithely, and so did I; which, no doubt, caused the new nurse
to be regarded as a light-minded sinner by the Chaplain, who
roamed vaguely about, with his hands in his pockets, preach-
ing resignation to cold, hungry, wounded men, and evidently
feeling himself, what he certainly was, the wrong man in the
wrong place.

"I say, Mrs.!" called a voice behind me; and, turning, I saw a
rough Michigander, with an arm blown off at the shoulder,
and two or three bullets still in him—as he afterwards mentioned, as carelessly as if gentlemen were in the habit of carrying such trifles about with them. I went to him, and while
administering a dose of soap and water, he whispered irefully:

"That red-headed devil, over yonder, is a reb, hang him!
He's got shot of a foot, or he'd cut like the rest of the lot. Don't
you wash him, nor feed him, but jest let him holler till he's
tired. It's a blasted shame to fetch them fellers in here, along
side of us; and so I'll tell the chap that bosses this concern;
cuss me if I don't."

I regret to say that I did not deliver a moral sermon upon
the duty of forgiving our enemies, and the sin of profanity,
then and there; but, being a red-hot Abolitionist, stared
fixedly at the tall rebel, who was a copperhead, in every sense
of the word, and privately resolved to soap his eyes, rub

his nose the wrong way, and excoriate his cuticle generally, if I had the washing of him.

My amiable intentions, however, were frustrated; for, when I approached with as Christian an expression as my principles would allow, and asked the question— "Shall I try to make you more comfortable, sir?" all I got for my pains was a gruff—

"No; I'll do it myself."

"Here's your Southern chivalry, with a witness," thought I, dumping the basin down before him, thereby quenching a strong desire to give him a summary baptism, in return for his ungraciousness; for my angry passions rose, at this rebuff, in a way that would have scandalized good Dr. Watts. He was a disappointment in all respects, (the rebel, not the blessed Doctor,) for he was neither fiendish, romantic, pathetic, or anything interesting; but a long, fat man, with a head like a burning bush, and a perfectly expressionless face: so I could dislike him without the slightest drawback, and ignored his existence from that day forth. One redeeming trait he certainly did possess, as the floor speedily testified; for his ablutions were so vigorously performed, that his bed soon stood like an isolated island, in a sea of soap-suds, and he resembled a dripping merman, suffering from the loss of a fin. If cleanliness is a near neighbor to godliness, then was the big rebel the godliest man in my ward that day.

Having done up our human wash, and laid it out to dry, the second syllable of our version of the word War-fare was enacted with much success. Great trays of bread, meat, soup and coffee appeared; and both nurses and attendants turned waiters, serving bountiful rations to all who could eat. I can call my pinafore to testify to my good will in the work, for in ten minutes it was reduced to a perambulating bill of fare, presenting samples of all the refreshments going or gone. It was a lively scene; the long room lined with rows of beds, each filled by an occupant, whom water, shears, and clean raiment, had transformed from a dismal ragamuffin into a recumbent hero, with a cropped head. To and fro rushed

matrons, maids, and convalescent "boys," skirmishing with
knives and forks; retreating with empty plates; marching and
countermarching, with unvaried success, while the clash of
busy spoons made most inspiring music for the charge of our
Light Brigade:

"Beds to the front of them
Beds to the right of them,
Beds to the left of them,
Nobody blundered.
Beamed at by hungry souls,
Screamed at with brimming bowls,
Steamed at by army rolls,
Buttered and sundered.
With coffee not cannon plied,
Each must be satisfied,
Whether they lived or died;
All the men wondered."

Very welcome seemed the generous meal, after a week of
suffering, exposure, and short commons; soon the brown faces
began to smile as food, warmth, and rest, did their pleasant
work; and the grateful "Thankee's" were followed by more
graphic accounts of the battle and retreat, than any paid
reporter could have given us. Curious contrasts of the tragic
and comic met one everywhere; and some touching as well as
ludicrous episodes, might have been recorded that day. A six
foot New Hampshire man, with a leg broken and perforated
by a piece of shell, so large that, had I not seen the wound,
I would have regarded the story as a Munchausenism, beck-
oned me to come and help him, as he could not sit up, and
both his bed and beard were getting plentifully anointed with
soup. As I fed my big nestling with corresponding mouthfuls,
I asked him how he felt during the battle.

"Well, 'twas my fust, you see, so I aint ashamed to say I was
a trifle flustered in the beginnin', there was such an allfired
racket; for ef there's anything I do spleen agin, it's noise. But

when my mate, Eph Sylvester, fell, with a bullet through his head, I got mad, and pitched in, licketty cut. Our part of the fight didn't last long; so a lot of us larked round Fredericksburg, and give some of them houses a pretty consid'able of a rummage, till we was ordered out of the mess. Some of our fellows cut like time; but I warn't a-goin to run for nobody; and, fust thing I knew, a shell bust, right in front of us, and I keeled over, feelin' as if I was blowed higher'n a kite. I sung out, and the boys come back for me, double quick; but the way they chucked me over them fences was a caution, I tell you. Next day I was most as black as that darkey yonder, lickin' plates on the sly. This is bully coffee, ain't it? Give us another pull at it, and I'll be obliged to you."

I did; and, as the last gulp subsided, he said with a rub of his old handkerchief over eyes as well as mouth:

"Look a here; I've got a pair a earbobs and a handkercher pin I'm a goin to give you, if you'll have them; for you're the very moral o' Lizy Sylvester, poor Eph's wife; that's why I signalled you to come over here. They aint much, I guess, but they'll do to memorize the rebs by."

Burrowing under his pillow, he produced a little bundle of what he called "truck," and gallantly presented me with a pair of earrings, each representing a cluster of corpulent grapes, and the pin a basket of astonishing fruit, the whole large and coppery enough for a small warming pan. Feeling delicate about depriving him of such valuable relics, I accepted the earrings alone, and was obliged to depart, somewhat abruptly when my friend stuck the warming pan in the bosom of his night-gown, viewing it with much complacency, and, perhaps some tender memory, in that rough heart of his, for the comrade he had lost.

Observing that the man next him had left his meal untouched, I offered the same service I had performed for his neighbor, but he shook his head.

"Thank you, ma'am; I don't think I'll ever eat again, for I'm shot in the stomach. But I'd like a drink of water, if you aint too busy."

I rushed away, but the water pails were gone to be refilled,
and it was some time before they reappeared. I did not forget
my patient patient, meanwhile, and, with the first mugful,
hurried back to him. He seemed asleep; but something in the
dried white face caused me to listen at his lips for a breath.
None came. I touched his forehead, it was cold; and then I
knew that, while he waited, a better nurse than I had given
him a cooler draught, and healed him with a touch. I laid the
sheet over the quiet sleeper, whom no noise could now dis-
turb; and, half an hour later, the bed was empty. It seemed a
poor requital for all he had sacrificed and suffered,—that hospital bed, lonely even in a crowd; for there was no familiar
face for him to look his last upon; no friendly voice to say,
Good bye; no hand to lead him gently down into the Valley of
the Shadow; and he vanished, like a drop in that red sea upon
whose shores so many women stand lamenting. For a
moment I felt bitterly indignant at this seeming carelessness of
the value of life, the sanctity of death; then consoled myself
with the thought that, when the great muster roll was called,
these nameless men might be promoted above many whose
tall monuments record the barren honors they have won.

All having eaten, drank, and rested, the surgeons began
their rounds; and I took my first lesson in the art of dressing
wounds. It wasn't a festive scene, by any means; for Dr. P.,
whose Aid I constituted myself, fell to work with a vigor
which soon convinced me that I was a weaker vessel, though
nothing could have induced me to confess it then. He had
served in the Crimea, and seemed to regard a dilapidated
body very much as I should have regarded a damaged gar-
ment; and, turning up his cuffs, whipped out a very unpleasant looking housewife, cutting, sawing, patching and piecing,
with the enthusiasm of an accomplished surgical seamstress;
explaining the process, in scientific terms, to the patient,
meantime; which, of course, was immensely cheering and
comfortable. There was an uncanny sort of fascination in
watching him, as he peered and probed into the mechanism of
those wonderful bodies, whose mysteries he understood so

❡ well. The more intricate the wound, the better he liked it.
A poor private, with both legs off, and shot through the lungs,
possessed more attractions for him than a dozen generals,
slightly scratched in some "masterly retreat"; and had any one
appeared in small pieces, requesting to be put together again,
he would have considered it a special dispensation.

The amputations were reserved till the morrow, and the
merciful magic of ether was not thought necessary that day, so
the poor souls had to bear their pains as best they might. It
is all very well to talk of the patience of woman; and far be it
from me to pluck that feather from her cap, for, heaven
knows, she isn't allowed to wear many; but the patient
endurance of these men, under trials of the flesh, was truly
wonderful. Their fortitude seemed contagious, and scarcely a
cry escaped them, though I often longed to groan for them,
when pride kept their white lips shut, while great drops stood
upon their foreheads, and the bed shook with the irrepressible
tremor of their tortured bodies. One or two Irishmen anathe-
matized the doctors with the frankness of their nation, and
ordered the Virgin to stand by them, as if she had been the
wedded Biddy to whom they could administer the poker, if
she didn't; but as a general thing, the work went on in silence,
broken only by some quiet request for roller, instruments,
or plaster, a sigh from the patient, or a sympathizing murmur
from the nurse.

It was long past noon before these repairs were even partially made; and, having got the bodies of my boys into something like order, the next task was to minister to their minds,
by writing letters to the anxious souls at home; answering   ❢
questions, reading papers, taking possession of money and
valuables; for the eighth commandmant was reduced to a
very fragmentary condition, both by the blacks and whites,
who ornamented our hospital with their presence. Pocket
books, purses, miniatures, and watches, were sealed up,
labelled, and handed over to the matron, till such times as the
owners thereof were ready to depart homeward or campward
again. The letters dictated to me, and revised by me, that

afternoon, would have made an excellent chapter for some
future history of the war; for, like that which Thackeray's
"Ensign Spooney" wrote his mother just before Waterloo, they
were "full of affection, pluck, and bad spelling"; nearly all
giving lively accounts of the battle, and ending with a somewhat sudden plunge from patriotism to provender, desiring
"Marm," "Mary Ann," or "Aunt Peters," to send along some
pies, pickles, sweet stuff, and apples, "to yourn in haste,"
Joe, Sam, or Ned, as the case might be.

My little Sergeant insisted on trying to scribble something
with his left hand, and patiently accomplished some half
dozen lines of hieroglyphics, which he gave me to fold and
direct, with a boyish blush, that rendered a glimpse of "My
Dearest Jane," unnecessary, to assure me that the heroic lad
had been more successful in the service of Commander-in-
Chief Cupid than that of Gen. Mars; and a charming little
romance blossomed instanter in Nurse Periwinkle's romantic
fancy, though no further confidences were made that day, for
Sergeant fell asleep, and, judging from his tranquil face,
visited his absent sweetheart in the pleasant land of dreams.

At five o'clock a great bell rang, and the attendants flew, not
to arms, but to their trays, to bring up supper, when a second
uproar announced that it was ready. The new comers woke at
the sound; and I presently discovered that it took a very bad
wound to incapacitate the defenders of the faith for the con-
sumption of their rations; the amount that some of them
sequestered was amazing; but when I suggested the probabil-
ity of a famine hereafter, to the matron, that motherly lady
cried out; "Bless their hearts, why shouldn't they eat? It's their
only amusement; so fill every one, and, if there's not enough
ready to-night, I'll lend my share to the Lord by giving it to
the boys." And, whipping up her coffee-pot and plate of toast,
she gladdened the eyes and stomachs of two or three dissatis-
fied heroes, by serving them with a liberal hand; and I haven't
the slightest doubt that, having cast her bread upon the
waters, it came back buttered, as another large-hearted old
lady was wont to say.

Then came the doctor's evening visit; the administration of
medicines; washing feverish faces; smoothing tumbled beds;
wetting wounds; singing lullabies; and preparations for
the night. By twelve, the last labor of love was done; the last
"good night" spoken; and, if any needed a reward for that
day's work, they surely received it, in the silent eloquence of
those long lines of faces, showing pale and peaceful in the
shaded rooms, as we quitted them, followed by grateful
glances that lighted us to bed, where rest, the sweetest, made
our pillows soft, while Night and Nature took our places,
filling that great house of pain with the healing miracles of
Sleep, and his divine brother, Death.

Alcott, Louisa May. *Hospital Sketches*. Boston: James Redpath
Publishers, 1863.

Reminiscences of an Army Nurse during the Civil War

by Adelaide W. Smith

PATRIOTISM TO THE Federal cause had a lock on the "City of Brooklyn" in Long Island, New York, from the very beginning of the war. Many regiments were raised in the city and the surrounding towns and villages, until it seemed that every young man between the ages of fifteen and eighteen was inducted into the armed forces.

There was an overwhelming popular enthusiastic zeal among the citizens in the area for the cause. All wished to pitch in and aid with patient labor or by liberal giving for the soldiers. At the news of the first battle, there was an outpouring of clothing, blankets, food, and hospital supplies. Each successive engagement brought forth a repeated flow of donations.

The Young Men's Christian Association, already an efficient organization, became a volunteer group delivering the donated supplies to the battlefronts for the ill and wounded troops. Soon other organizations appeared to assist in the moving of emergency supplies and to care for the wounded.

After the great battles of the summer and fall of 1862, large numbers of disabled troops were brought to Brooklyn for care and treatment. At one time three hospitals—Long Island College Hospital, Fort Schuyler Hospital, and David's Island on the Sound—were full of ill and wounded soldiers.

When men arrived from the battlefields, they needed everything from medical care to clothes, blankets, and bedding. Benevolent women of the city formed committees and visited hospitals to see what supplies were necessary, then stocked them properly. Still, there occasionally was unequal distribution. Other women offered to work in the wards to give care and comfort to the battle casualties, yet there were times when the greed of hospital administrators interfered with patient care.

Adelaide W. Smith was an independent volunteer who offered her services at the beginning of the mass effort to help at hospitals. Her book about her wartime experiences, Reminiscences of an Army Nurse during the Civil War, *carries the following dedication:*

To the Boys in Blue 1861–1865;
and to those brave women, who, with smiling faces and breaking hearts, sent them forth to save their country and their homes, while they themselves toiled in fields and elsewhere, waiting to welcome home too many who never returned; and to that band of heroic devoted women, many of whom left luxurious homes for the discomforts and privations of hospital life, and died, self-sacrificing patriots of the war, this true story is affectionately dedicated.
Adelaide W. Smith

In July, 1862, one hundred and twenty-five patients from the Army of the Potomac were sent to the Long Island College Hospital. No adequate preparation had been made to provide for these sick men. Through the press a public call was sent out for volunteers. Many ladies and gentlemen at once offered to help care for the sick, and to supply food for their emaciated bodies.

Watches of four hours each during the day were assigned to the women, and at night the same number of hours were allotted to men volunteers.

Owing to the astonishing liberality of the citizens of Brooklyn, the hospital donations seemed like a great cornucopia overflowing the larders of the improvised kitchen. Tender, motherly care, combined with the best of diet, at once restored many a poor, hungry homesick boy. Most of them recovered and returned to their regiments or were sent home.

My first patient was a bright, cheerful young man, Allan Foote, of Michigan, who had been dangerously wounded by a shot that passed through the left lung and out at his back. Such wounds were then supposed to be fatal. He was, however, convalescent, and later was discharged. When he returned to his home in Michigan he again enlisted, raised a company, and went out once more to the front as a captain. This time he served till the end of the war, when he returned to his native State safe and well.

A lady, wishing to say something flattering of him to a visitor, remarked: "Why, he was shot right in his back." Seeing the boy wince at this innocent imputation, I explained that he had received that shot in the breast while facing the enemy in battle.

Among many incidents of his early army life, Allan Foote told me the following:

"I shall never forget his expression when my father gave his written consent to my enlistment in the army in April of '61, as he handed it to me and said, while tears were running down his cheeks, 'My son, do your duty, die if it must be, but never prove yourself a coward.' We can hardly imagine at what cost that was given, and it is now a source of much satisfaction to me to know that God in His mercy so guided me while in the service that no action of mine has ever caused a pain to my father's heart, and when I returned at the close of the war he seemed as proud of my scars as I was."

John Sherman was a remarkable case of lost identity. He was eighteen years of age, six feet in height, with broad shoulders and a Washingtonian head, and seemed like some great prone statue as he lay perfectly helpless but for one hand,—a gentle fair-haired boy to whom we became much attached. He was evidently refined, and perfectly clear on religious and political subjects. Though without a wound he had been completely paralyzed by concussion caused by a cannon. He could take only infant's food and drank milk, which was all the nourishment he could retain. The mystery was that he claimed to come from Cattaraugus County, N. Y., but when I wrote letters to every possible locality, nothing could be learned of such a boy; nor could the officers of his regiment trace him during this time. Some scamp who claimed to come from his town, was admitted through the carelessness of the hospital attendants, and so deceived the poor boy that he gave him ninety dollars army pay just received, to send home to his father. Of course the scamp was never heard of again. My theory is that he enlisted under an assumed name and town, and had, after the concussion, forgotten his real name and identity. He was sent to the Fifty-second Street hospital, where I saw him a year later, walking alone and quite well,—a finely developed physical form. Though he knew me, he held to his old statement. Later he was cruelly persuaded to ask for a discharge which left him homeless, with no refuge but the poor house.

Soldiers' homes were then unknown; and I fear that, at least for a while, he was cared for as a pauper. About this time I went to the "field work" and lost sight of him, though I have often wondered what his fate has been.

A miserably thin, gaunt boy, whom we knew as "Say", came under my observation. He was never satisfied, though he ate enormously, and whenever we passed through his ward he invariably shouted: "Say! ye ain't got no pie nor cake, nor cheese, nor nuthin', hev ye?" When he reached home, his father, a farmer, sent to the hospital the largest cheese I ever saw. This the men all craved; but it was a luxury denied them by the doctors. Patients often had it smuggled in. One poor fellow was found dead, one morning, with a package of cheese under his pillow.

In another ward poor Isaac was slowly dying of dysentery, gasping for a drink of cool water, which the rules of the profession at that day denied to such patients. Day after day he lay helpless, while a large water cooler dripped constantly day and night before his feverish eyes and parched body.

One day he called to me and said: "Won't you please sit on my cot so I can rest my knees against your back? They are so tired and I can't hold them up,"—poor fleshless bones that had no weight. Somewhat relieved while I sat there he went on: "Now, Miss Smith, you think I am dying, don't you?"

"Well, Isaac," I replied hesitatingly," we fear you are."

Then with all the strength of his poor skeleton body, he exclaimed, "O then, give me a drink of water that I may die easier. You know I am dying, so it can do no harm."

Could I refuse a dying man a drink of water, even in the face of orders? He wanted "just a pint." Watching my chance I went quickly to the cooler and brought a glass of cool water. With unnatural strength he raised himself and, reaching out for the glass, grasped it and swallowed the water with one great gulp. Then returning the empty glass he cried: "There, that was just half! O, give me the other half." This I did, rather fearfully. After greedily drinking the water he dropped back with a sigh of relief, saying—"Now I can die easy." I arranged quietly with my patients in the ward so that he could have water as long as he lived; but not many days after I found his empty cot.

The hospital at that time, was little known, being quite obscured under the limitations of two conservative, retrogressive old doctors, who showed no favor or sympathy for the sick men, and seemed to see them only as probably "subjects."

Many just protests from the kindly women workers were utterly disregarded by these doctors. Dr. Colton, a handsome young man then an interne, though not of age or yet graduated, found himself often between the "upper and nether millstones" of the urgency of volunteer workers, and the immovable, implacable heads of the hospital. Dr. Colton, now a successful retired physician, occupies a prominent position in this hospital, which in late years, is ranked among the very best of Brooklyn's institutions.

Meanwhile the people grew tired of the continual demand for

supplies, toward which the hospital contributed very little,
though it drew regularly from the government "rations" in the
form of thirty-seven cents per day for each man. Consequently
public contributions became very meagre.

Then in the autumn came ninety-one sick and wounded soldiers, who stood—or dropped—on the grass plots surrounding
the hospital while waiting to be enrolled. A procession of grey
skeletons, they were ghastly, dirty, famished, with scarcely the
semblance of men. One of them stared at me rather sharply and,
seeing that I observed it, said, "Excuse me, ma'am, I haven't
seen a white woman before in many months an' it seems good to
look at you."

It became difficult to get proper food in the hospital for the
men. Some of the volunteers, like myself, could still give their
whole time and thought gratuitously, and we continued bringing
supplies from our homes for special cases. My mother sent gal-
lons of shell clam juice,—the most healing of all natural tonics
when boiled in the shell,—which became popular in the hospital.
My mother also invited companies of four or five convalescents
at a time to "a good square meal," when they always chose for
their suppers, coffee, buckwheat cakes and sausages. Two gal-
lons of batter would become hot cakes; and it took the combined
help of the whole family and the cook to keep them supplied;
but the hungry boys were at last satisfied and happy. I had
no difficulty in obtaining passes for them, as they felt in honor
bound to return promptly to the hospital.

One poor fellow, dying of typhoid, was so irritable and pro-
fane to the ignorant, heartless men nurses of the hospital, that
they would not care for him during the night. Realizing that the
end was near, and feeling certain that he would otherwise die
alone, I decided one night to remain with him until his last
breath. Just before he died, even while the pallor of death over-
spread his face, he struck at the nurse whom I had compelled to
stay near him. At last the poor dying man gasped: "Lift me up
higher! higher! higher!!" We raised the poor skeleton as high as
we could reach—and it was all over. His family refused his
body, saying, "He was no good to us in life, why should we bury
him?" It is not difficult to imagine that his home influences had
been unfavorable to the development of moral character.

Some months later, being almost the only young woman still visiting the hospital, I felt obliged to report to that rarely good man, Mr. McMullen,—whose benevolence and generosity had at first brought the patients to the hospital and to the care of the people,—neglect of soldiers, who were then treated like charity patients. He immediately reported these conditions to the medical department, and the men were removed to the government hospitals, which were by this time systematized and in good running order.

After the patients had been transferred from the Long Island College Hospital, I secured a pass on the steamboat Thomas P. Way, to visit hospitals of the "Department of the East," in charge of Surgeon McDougall, a thorough disciplinarian, and a just, kind man.

David's Island, on the Sound, had a finely conducted hospital, with a diet kitchen in charge of ladies. There I saw hundreds of well-fed, happy Confederate patients, so many, indeed that they could not be supplied at once with proper clothing, and so made a unique appearance as they walked about in dressing gowns, white drawers, and slippers. They were soon to be exchanged for our own poor skeleton "Boys" who were coming home slowly and painfully, some dying on the way, to be met by kindly hands and aching hearts eagerly awaiting them.

Fort Schuyler Hospital, on the East River, was formed like a wheel, the hub being headquarters and the spokes extending into wards for patients. One young man of much refinement had been at one of our home suppers, and afterwards the company made a pact that if we were alive one year from that date we should hear each from the other. He exclaimed—"Dead or alive, you shall hear from me!" Being a spiritualist he believed this possible. He was sent to Fort Schuyler and one month later died of small pox. At the appointed date and hour a year later, I thought of this pact and tried to put myself in a receptive state. I did not, however, see him nor feel any manifestation of his spirit.

Smith, Adelaide W. *Reminiscences of an Army Nurse during the Civil War.* New York: Greaves Publishing Company, 1911.

Hospital Transports

*A Memoir of the Embarkation
of the Sick and Wounded
from the Peninsula of Virginia
in the Summer of 1862*

*Compiled and Published at the Request
of the Sanitary Commission
by Frederick Law Olmstead*

THE SANITARY COMMISSION, *the forerunner of the American Red Cross, was an all-purpose welfare agency organized in New York in 1861 by Clara Barton and a group of volunteers. In the beginning it enlisted doctors to investigate sanitation in army camps. Men and women soon joined the Commission to help distribute medical supplies, food, and clothes. They also looked after soldier's dependents, worked as nurses and aides in hospitals, and raised funds by conducting auctions of goods donated by farmers and manufacturers.*

Some of the younger and feistier women went into the field. They served at army hospitals, at the battlefront, and at post infirmaries and clinics. Others ran trains and hospital ships.

One branch, Hospital Transports, received little notice during the war. The Commission, wanting to tell its story, published a quantity of letters and other papers containing observations made on the spot by those in its service who assisted in the embarkation and care of the sick and wounded on the peninsula of Virginia in 1862.

Passages from these were selected and arranged in the book Hospital Transports *with a view to giving as many particulars as may be necessary to illustrate the scope of the enterprise and the position it held as an aid to the government. (A similar service in the western rivers the same year was larger in scope and more satisfactory in some of its arrangements.)*

The letters quoted here were for the most part addressed to intimate friends, with no thought that they could ever go beyond them. Nearly all of them were written hastily, often with a pencil, while passing in a boat from one vessel to another. The entire collection was written by two officers of the Commission and six ladies serving with them, and the same occurrences are often described from more than one point of view. As the different writers are quoted in succession, a capital letter at the head of a paragraph will indicate the change from one writer to another. The officers will be known by the letters A and B, and the ladies by M and N.

Among the surgeons who freely gave their aid in the enterprise were numbered some of the leading members of the profession, in general terms. The class termed "ward-masters" was mainly composed of medi-

cal students of two years, with some young men of Philadelphia who had previous experience in caring for sick soldiers in the local charities of that city. It also included some students of theology. The responsibility for the detail of care of the patients lay chiefly with this class.

A sudden transfer of the scene of active war early in the summer of 1862, from the high banks of the Potomac to a low, swampy region among a network of rivers and creeks, required appliances for the proper care of the sick and wounded that did not appear to have been contemplated in the government arrangements. Seeing this, with the approval of the Medical Bureau, a proposal was made to the quartermaster general to allow the Sanitary Commission to take in hand some of the transport steamboats of his department, of which a large number were at that time lying idle, to fit them up and furnish them suitably in all respects for the reception and care of sick and wounded men, providing surgeons and other necessary attendants, without cost to the government. After tedious delays and disappointments of various kinds—one fine, large boat having been assigned partially furnished by the Commission and then withdrawn—an order was at length received, authorizing the Commission to take possession of any of the government transports not in actual use that might be at that time lying at Alexandria. The only available vessel built well enough to withstand the ocean voyage from Virginia to New York or Boston was the Daniel Webster, *an old Pacific Coast steamer of small capacity. She recently had been used for transporting troops and had been "stripped of everything movable but dirt," so the labor of adapting her to the purpose of moving the sick was not light.*

This vessel was assigned to the Commission on April 25. Provisional engagements previously had been made, in New York and Philadelphia, with the persons afterward employed as her hospital company. The moment the order was received, these persons were telegraphed for, and the refitting of the ship began. At this point begins their story.[1]

---

[1] The compiler and publisher of this work, Frederick Law Olmstead, was a successful landscape architect designing such areas as Prospect Park and Central Park in New York City. He was also a sensitive writer and was sent on assignment by *The New York Times* to write about blacks in the South. His columns were so well received that they were produced as books (1850-1861). In 1861 he was called upon to become executive secretary of the newly formed Sanitary Commission.

Hospital Transport, **Daniel Webster,**
Cheeseman's Creek, April 30, 1862

(A.) I received General Meig's order under which this ship
came into our hands on Friday. She was then at Alexandria,
and could not be got over the shoals to Washington. It was not
till near night that I was able to get a lighter, and this, after
one trip, was taken off to carry reinforcements to McDowell at
Fredericksburg. I succeeded before daylight of Saturday in
getting a tug at work, and by the next morning, Sunday, had
her hold full. At eleven o'clock got the hospital company on
board, but the commissaries failed in their engagements, and
at last I had to send off a foraging-party at Alexandria for
beef. Finally at four o'clock, D., who had gone after E., and E,
who had gone after beef, arrive simultaneously from different
directions. With E. came the beef, and we at once got under
way.

We had six medical students, twenty men nurses (volunteers all), four surgeons, four ladies, a dozen contrabands
(field hands),[2] three carpenters, and half a dozen miscella-
neous passengers. There were, besides, five of us members of
the Sanitary Commission and of the central staff, with one of
the Philadelphia associates, eight military officers, ninety soldiers (convalescents, returning to their regiments), some quartermaster's mechanics, and a short ship's crew and officers.
The ship has a house aft, with state-rooms for thirty, and an
old-fashioned packet-saloon below, with state-rooms opening
out of it; and all forward of the engine-rooms, a big steerage,
or "tween decks," which had been fitted with shelves, some of
them fifteen feet deep, in which the soldiers had been carried
to the Peninsula, packed in layers.

I organized all our Commission people at sunset on Sunday,
in two watches, sea-fashion; appointed watch-officers, and
have worked since, night and day, refitting ship. We broke up
all the transport arrangements,—they were in a filthy condi-

---

[2] (Original author's note) Slaves that were abandoned during the advance of the
Union armies were handled in the same manner as confiscated cattle and corn—as
contraband liable to be held or used by the Union forces.

tion,—thoroughly scraped, washed, and scrubbed the whole ship from stem to stern, inside and out; whitewashed the steerage; knocked away the bulkheads of the wings of the engine room section, so as to get a thorough draft from stern to stern; then set to fitting and furnishing new bunks; started a new house on deck, forward; made and fitted an apothecary's shop; and when we arrived at Cheeseman's Creek were ready for patients.

(M.) It was a bright day, the river peaceful and shining. Just as we started, the little gunboat, *Yankee* passed up, bringing, all on a string, five rebel craft which she had just taken in the Rappahannock. Late in the afternoon we passed the "stone fleet," eight boats, all ready to sink in the channel, in case the *Merrimack* should try to run up the Potomac. The rebels having taken up all the buoys, at dark we had come to anchor.

Sunday, the first day, was gone. As for us, we had spent it, sitting on deck, sewing upon a hospital flag, fifteen by eight, and singing hymns to take the edge off this secular occupation. Just after we had anchored, a chaplain was discovered among the soldiers; and in half an hour we got together for service, and an "unprepared" discourse upon charity, much like unprepared discourses in general. Quite another thing was the singing of the contrabands, who all came in and stood in a row so black, at the dark end of the cabin, that I could see neither eyes nor teeth. But they sang heartily, and everybody followed them.

(A.) *Cheeseman's Creek.*—I went ashore to report our arrival to the Medical Director. On our way up the harbor,—a shallow river-mouth, with low, pine-covered banks, in which there are now about four hundred steamboats and small transport-craft,—I hailed the steamboat *Daniel Webster* No. 2, which carries the ———— Regiment New York Volunteers, and let the Colonel know that his wife was among our nurses. This morning I received his acknowledgements in the form of a check for $1,000 for the Commission, accompanied by what was still better, a note of the most hearty and appreciative recognition of what the Commission had done for the relief of the soldiers.

Picking our way among all the craft, and keeping out of
the way of the tugs and tenders which were flying about, we
landed on a large meadow where were a number of wall-
tents, one labelled "Office of Quartermaster's Department";
another, "Telegraph Office"; another, "Post-Office"; another,
"Office of Land Transportation"; another, "Harbor-Master,"
&c, &c. One contained a number of prisoners, brought in the
day before, and, of course, well-guarded. Ordnance and forage barges lay along the shore, with a few big guns, and piles
of shot and shell, just landed. The ground was crowded;—
orderlies holding horses; lounging, dirty soldiers; killers and
fatigue-parties at work in relays; sentries; Quartermaster's
people, white and black; and a hundred army wagons loaded
with forage and biscuit-boxes from the barges. I went at once
to Colonel Ingalls, at the Quartermaster's office. He was kind,
prompt, decisive; horses were ordered for us, and we soon
rode off through a swamp forest, the air full of the roar of
falling trees and the shouts of teamsters and working-parties
of soldiers, the former trying to navigate their wagons, and
the latter making corduroy roads for them. The original
country roads had all been used up; it was difficult even to
ford across them, when we had occasion to do so, on horseback. The army wagons, each drawn by six mules, and with
very light loads, were jerked about frightfully. We passed
many wrecks, and some horses which had sunk and been
smothered. Some wagons were loaded with gun-beds and
heavy rope screens for embrasures; and we saw eight or ten
mortars, each on a truck by itself, and drawn by from sixteen
to twenty-four horses. At the first open ground we found cavalry exercising; then a cavalry camp, then a bit of wood, then
rising dry ground, and our road ran through more camps.
Then, coming in the midst of these camps, to the crest of a low
swell, we opened suddenly a grand view of the valley of York
River, a country something like the valley of the Raritan, at
Eagleswood and opposite, but with less wood, more piny and
more diversified, the river much broader, a mile and a half,
perhaps across. On the slope before us—nearly flat, with an
inclination toward the river—was a space of several hundred
acres, clear land, and a camp for some twenty to forty thousand men; shelter-tents, and all alive. It was a magnificent

scene, the camp and all beyond, as we came upon it suddenly—right into it, at full gallop. The military "effect" was
heightened now and then by a crashing report of artillery.

In the midst of the camp we came upon a long rack,—a pole
on crotched sticks,—at which were fastened a score or more
of horses. "We must stop here," said Dr. C. "They don't let
you ride in." And that was all to show that we had reached
Headquarters.

It was an aristocratic quarter of the town, when you came to
look at the clean tents and turf, but there were no flags or
signs to distinguish it. We walked to the tent of the Medical
Director, and just then there came another of those crashing
reports. "They have been keeping that up all night," said the
Doctor. "That isn't the enemy?" "O yes! we are quite within
range here."

The medical arrangements seem to be deplorably insuffi-
cient. The Commission is at this time actually distributing
daily of hospital supplies much more than the government.

(**B.**) *May 1st.* No patients on board yet; ship getting a final pol-
ish. Got up early and found the *Elizabeth* coming alongside for
stores. The Commission has here at present, besides the *Daniel
Webster*, one or two store-ships, and the *Wilson Small*, a boat
of light draught, fitted up as a little hospital, to run up creeks
and bring down sick and wounded to the transports. She is
under the care of Dr. C., and has her little supply of hospital
clothing, beds, food, &c., always ready for chance service.
There is also a well-supplied storehouse ashore.

In sight are the abandoned rebel quarters at Shipping Point,
now used as hospitals by one of our divisions; a number of
log-huts finely built, but on low and filthy ground, surrounded by earthworks, which are rained on half the time and
fiercely shone on the other half, and from which are exhaling
deadly vapors all the time, a death-place for scores of our men
who are piled in there, covered with vermin, dying with their
uniforms on and collars up,—dying of fever. . . .

I attended this afternoon to the systematic arrangement of
the commissariat stores down aft, sent a telegram for more
supplies to Baltimore, arranged for stowing the contrabands
and putting bunks in the new deck-ward, and then put two

ladies and a nice supply of oranges, tea, lemons, wine, &c.,
&c. on a small boat, and started them with ———— to Ship
Point Hospital, where four poor fellows died last night. Of
course there is that vitally important medical etiquette to
observe, here as elsewhere, and we must approach carefully,
when we would not frustrate our own plans;—and so it is.
"————, suppose you go ashore and ask whether it will be
agreeable to have the ladies come over and visit the hospital,—just to walk through and talk with the men." So the
ladies have gone "to talk with the men," with spirit-lamps,
and farina, and lemons, and brandy, and clean clothes, and
expect to have an improving conversation. After the party
was off, sent order to Fort Monroe for special supplies;
received Dr. Tripler who dined with us; furnished wine, tea,
bread, to a surgeon who had been told that the Commission's
flag was flying here, and had come seven miles across the
swamps, and rowed out to us in a small boat to try for these
things.

(M.) By dark the *Wilson Small* came alongside with our first
patients, thirty-five in number, who were carefully lifted on
board and swung through the hatches on their stretchers. In
half an hour they had all been tea'd and coffeed and refreshed
by the nurse, and shortly after were all undressed and put to
bed clean and comfortable, and in a droll state of grateful
wonder; the bad cases of fever furnished with sponges and
cologne-water for bathing, and wine and water or brandy-
toddy for drinking, and a man to watch them, and ward-
master up and down the wards, and a young doctor in the
apothecary's shop, and today (May 3d) they are all better. . . .

Meantime additional supplies arrived from Washington,
Baltimore, and Fortress Monroe, and a surgeon and nurses of
our company were busy daily on shore at the Ship Point Hospital, dispensing stores, and doing what they could for the
poor fellows there, who seemed to us in want of everything. . . .
One hundred and ninety patients have now come on board;
eighteen miles some of them say they have been brought in
the ambulances (large statement of exhausted fellows jolted
over corduroy roads).

We ladies arrange our days into three watches, and then a

promiscuous one for any of us, as the night work may
demand, after eight o'clock. Take Sunday, for instance.

It was ———'s and ———'s watch from seven to twelve. So
they were up and had hot breakfast ready in our pantry,
which is amidships between the forward and aft ward; ward-
masters on the port and starboard sides for each ward, to
watch the distribution of the food, and no promiscuous rushing about allowed; the number for coffee and the number for
tea marked in the ward diet-books under the head of Breakfast, and the number for house-diet, or for beef-tea and toddy,
&c., marked also; so that when the Hospital company learns
to count straight,—an achievement of some difficulty, apparently,—there will be no opportunity for confusion. After
breakfast we all assembled in the forward or sickest ward, and
Dr. G. read the simple prayers for those at sea and for the sick.
Our whole company and all the patients were together. It was
good to have the service then and there. Our poor sick fellows
lay all about us in their beds and listened quietly. As the
prayer for the dying was finished, a soldier close by the doctor
had ended his strife.

After twelve, our watch came on, and till four we gave out
clean clothes, handkerchiefs, cologne, clothes to the nurses,
and served the dinner, consulting the diet-books again. The
house-diet which was all distributed from our pantry, was
nice thick soup and rice-pudding, and we made, over our
spirit lamps, the beef tea and gruels for special cases. So with
little cares came four o'clock, and with it clean hands and our
own dinner; after which the other two ladies came on for the
last watch, which included tea. Then there was beef-tea and
punch to be made for use during the night; and so the day for
us ended with our sitting in the pantry and talking over
evils to be remedied, and should the soiled clothes be sewed
up in canvas-bags and trailed behind the ship, or hung at the
stern, or headed up in barrels and steam washed when the
ship got in. We crawled up into our bunks that night amid a
tremendous firing of big guns, and woke up in the morning to
the announcement that Yorktown was evacuated.

(M.) While we were lying anchored off Ship Point, down in
the Gulf, New Orleans had surrendered quietly, and round

the corner from us Fort Macon had been taken. What was it all to us, so long as the beef-tea was ready at the right moment?

(A.) *May 5th.* On Sunday the *Ocean Queen,* coming up from Old Point, grounded about five miles off the harbor, and I went down and put a few beds and men on board to assume a footing. She had been brought to Old Point with the intention of using her to amuse the *Merrimack,* and had therefore been stripped of everything not necessary to the subsistence of the small crew.

(M.) On the way back at eight in the evening, found that a great part of the army fleet, three hundred or more steamboats full of life, all before scattered for miles about the harbor, had been collected in close order and steam up. A number of heavy steamers swept past also, each with a tow a quarter of a mile long, making on the dark evening a long line of light and life. It was strange to see these floating cities melt away; the colored lights from the rigging going out one by one, and the bands and bugle calls growing faint and far.

(A.) I had sent the *Webster* to sea, and with Mrs. ——— and sister, B., and some two or three others, started in the *Small* to go to the telegraph and mail, and to bury the body of a patient who had died in the night. It was raining hard. When we reached the shore there was no post-office, no telegraph,— nothing of the military station left, except some wagons and transports. Our storehouse was a mile back. I left a portion of our party to move the goods from it on board the barge, and started in the *Small* for Yorktown, to which I presumed Head-quarters would have been moved. On getting out of the har-bor, we saw that the *Queen* was under way. It turned out that she had been ordered to Yorktown by the Harbor-Master. As she was lying-to, to sound the channel, we came up with her, and I went on board, after which—the *Small* going ahead to feel the way—we had a magnificent sail to Yorktown, the river so full of vessels that it was like getting up the Thames, only the lead was constantly going, "By the mark, five! A quarter less six!" and so on. Noble river! and a noble ship! Ahead, above all the fleet of three hundred transports, there were a dozen men of war. With our hospital flag at the fore, we slowly but boldly passed through the squadron, and came to anchor, the biggest ship of all, in the advance,—only one gunboat, as a picket guard, being above us. I went ashore with the Captain and the young men, but could find no telegraph, and no officer of the general staff; and as many men had been killed and wounded by the torpedo-traps,—infernal machines set by the rebels,—we were not allowed to enter the fortified lines of Yorktown. So, picking up a hospital cot and stretcher left by the enemy, I took boat again to return to the ship, leaving the Captain and others ashore. As I pulled out through the vessels at the wharf, I saw to my surprise two small "stern-wheel" steamboats coming alongside the *Queen*, one on each side. Hastening on board, I found that these boats were loaded with sick men, whom an officer in charge was about to throw off upon the *Queen*. They were the sick of regiments which had been ordered suddenly forward last night, and which were at this very moment engaged in the battle of Williamsburg; we could hear the roar of artillery. They had been sent during the night by ambulances to the shore of Wormley's Creek, where a large number had been left, the officer assured me, lying on the ground in the rain, without food or attendance. His orders were to take them upon the "stern-wheelers," as many as both could carry, find the *Ocean Queen*, and put them upon her. I protested. The *Queen* at present was a mere hulk, without beds, bedding, or food even for her crew, and without a surgeon. It was obvious that the men were, many of them, very ill. Some were, in fact, in a dying state.

They were largely typhoid-fever patients; and having been for twenty-four hours without nourishment, wet from exposure to the storm, and many of them racked by the motion of the ambulances over those frightful swamp corduroy roads (which I described the other day) into delirium, I was sure that many would die if they long failed to receive most careful medical treatment, with stimulants, nourishment, and warmth, no one of which could at that time be got for them on the *Queen*. The officer, however, insisted. I determined to go ashore to look for a surgeon, or if possible to find Colonel Ingalls, the transport quartermaster, a gentleman, and a most energetic and sagacious officer. I put the two ship's officers each at a gangway, with instructions to let no one come on board till I returned, and to use force, if necessary. I found a surgeon—a civilian—who was willing to help us, and pulled back, finding to my disgust, when I reached the ship, that the miserable first officer had given way, and every man who could walk of the patients had been taken on board. The glorious women had hunted out a barrel containing some Indian meal from some dark place where it had been lost sight of, in the depths of the ship, and were already ladling out hot gruel, which they had made of it; and the poor, pale, emaciated, shivering wretches were lying anywhere, on the cabin floors, crying with sobbing, trembling voices, "God bless you, Miss! God bless you!" as it was given to them from the ship's deck-buckets. I never saw such misery or such gratitude. My rebel stretcher came at once in play, and, after distributing forty dollars among the half-mutinous superstitious, beastly Portugese crew and pantry servants, I got them at work bringing on the patients who were too feeble to be led on board. It was a slow tedious process. By the blessing of God, before it was over, B., with Dr. Ware,—the two very best men I ever saw for such an emergency,—came with the *Elizabeth*, and the Captain's authority soon added all the ship's force to the working party on her, filling beds and hoisting out bales of blankets. B. went on ashore, found a rebel cow at pasture, shot her, and brought off the beef with another surgeon. By ten o'clock at night every sick man was in a warm bed, and had received medical treatment; and beef-tea and milk-punch had been served to all who required it. But for three of them, even the women could do nothing but pray, and close their eyes.

At half past ten, I went aboard the *Small*, intending to run to fortress Monroe for additional supplies. It was stormy and thick, and I could not induce the Captain to go out till daylight. We reached Old Point about nine A.M. I got breakfast in the hotel, and then to Head-quarters. While in the telegraph room, a message was received, which was whispered between the operators; a minute afterwards a gun was fired, and the long roll beat; the infantry fell in on the parade, the artillery hurried to the ramparts and manned the heavy guns, and powder-carts were moving up the inclines. I asked, "What's all this?" "Telegram from Newport News that the *Merrimack* is coming out!" She did not come beyond Sewall's Point, however.

The boat from Baltimore brought six excellent New York surgeons, twenty-six nurses, and ten surgical dressers (medical students). I got them all on the *Small*, and having succeeded in obtaining the more important supplies in limited quantities, at noon left for Yorktown. On reaching here we found the "stern-wheelers" again alongside, and over three hundred patients on board; many very sick indeed, some delirious, some comatose, some fairly *in articulo*. The assistant surgeons, left behind at the abandoned camps, are too anxious to be rid of them, so as to move with their regiments, and have surgery of war. And as their orders authorize it, they hurry them off to us in this style, after a day's ride in army wagons, without springs, over such a country without roads as I described last week. They were horribly filthy, and there was no time to clean them, often not to undress them, as sick and fainting, they were lifted on board.

About noon the next day I completed a hospital organization of such forces as I had, dividing the cabins and the upper steerage of the ship into five wards, for the bad cases, each ward having one surgeon, two ward-masters, and four nurses, — the two latter classes in watches; besides these, some assistant nurses and servants, convalescent soldiers, and contrabands. In these wards only the very sick—chiefly cases of typhoid fever—were taken. By cutting away bulkheads, and getting windsails rigged, they were fairly well ventilated. I had to offer $200 for the repair of damages before this could be secured, however. All the rest of the ship was the sixth ward, in which the hernias, rheumatisms, bronchitises, lame and worn-out men were placed, organized in squads of fifty each, with a squad-master to draw their rations of house-diet.

To get proper food for all, decently cooked and distributed, has given me more concern than anything else. The ship servants are brutes, and our supply of utensils was cruelly short. Fortunately the Captain is a good-hearted and resolute man, and the ladies—God knows what we should have done without them!—have contrived to make some chafing-dishes with which the kitchen is pieced out wonderfully. Just think of

it for a moment. Here were one hundred miserably sick and
dying men, forced upon us before we had been an hour on
board; and tug after tug swarming round the great ship,
before we had a nail out of a box, and when there were but
ten pounds of Indian meal and two spoons to feed them with.
No account could do justice to the faithful industry of the
medical students, and young men; how we all got through
with it, I hardly know; but one idea is distinct,—that every
man had a good place to sleep in, and something hot to
eat daily, and that the sickest had every essential that could
have been given them in their own homes. . . .

B. was all this time driving everything to obtain supplies,
while the sick kept coming faster than we could get anything
ready for them. The last thing essential was more beef. B. at
length got hold of a couple of draught cattle of Franklin's
division, left behind in their advance by steamboats, and
while these were being killed and dressed, we filled up to
nine hundred patients.

To avoid having more pushed on board, I had the Captain
heave short; so the moment that B.'s boat came, and the beef
could be hoisted up, the steamer was under way, and before
night, no doubt, was well out to sea.

I then went on board the *Small* to drop down, quite ill for
the time from want of sleep and from fatigue. A few hours'
rest and a quiet dinner brought me all right, however, and at
sunset I set out with B. to look after the sick aboard.

One of the strange effects upon all concerned as workers on
these hospital ships, in the heart of all misery and pain, and
part of it, seems to have been the quieting of all excitement of
feeling and of expression,—a sort of apparent stoicism
granted for the occasion. A slight illustration of this quietness,
which was characteristic of most of the hospital party, is given
in the following passage from a letter of one of the ladies on
the *Ocean Queen*:—

"It seems a strange thing that the sight of such misery, such
death in life, should have been accepted by us all so quietly as
it was. We were simply eyes and hands for those three days.
Great, strong men were dying about us; in nearly every ward
some one was going. Yesterday one of the students called me
to go with him and say whether I had taken the name of a

dead man in the forward cabin the day he came in. He was a strong, handsome fellow, raving mad when brought in, and lying now, the day after, with pink cheeks, and peaceful look. I had tried to get his name, and once he seemed to understand and screeched out at the top of his voice, 'John H. Miller,' but whether it was his own name or that of some friend he wanted, I don't know; we could not find out. All the record I had of him was from my diet-list; 'Miller,—forward cabin, port side, number 119. Beef-tea and punch.'

"Last night Dr. Ware came to me to know how much floor-room we had. The immense saloon of the aft cabin was filled with mattresses so thickly placed that there was hardly stepping-room between them, and as I swung my lantern along the rows of pale faces, it showed me another strong man dead. N. had been working hard over him, but it was useless. He opened his eyes when she called 'Henry' clearly in his ear, and gave her a chance to pour brandy down his throat; but all did no good; he died quietly while she was helping some one else, and my lantern showed him gone. We are changed by all this contact with terror, else how could I deliberately turn my lantern on his face, and say to the doctor behind me, 'Is that man dead?' and then stand cooly while he examined him, listened, and pronounced him 'dead.' I could not have quietly said a year ago, "That will make one more bed, then, Doctor.' Sick men were waiting on deck in the cold, though, and every few feet of cabin floor were precious. So they took the dead man out, and put him to sleep in his coffin on deck. We had to climb over another soldier lying up there quiet as he, to get at the blankets to keep the living warm."

The business of feeding men by hundreds at short notice, in confined spaces, and with the aid of very limited cooking facilities, is one which can hardly be appreciated by those who have only heard, not seen, how it is accomplished. It takes good heads as well as good hearts, strong will as well as strong limbs, to avoid ruinous confusion. After a battle, when men are brought in so rapidly that they have to be piled in almost without reference to their being human beings, and every one raving for drink first and then for nourishment, it requires strong nerves to be able to attend to them properly. Habit and system are the two great aids,—or rather system

first of all, if possible; though system in such cases grows out
of experience. Happily system has ruled in the work of the
Sanitary Commission, and such success as has attended its
operations is chiefly due to this, as every one must have
observed who had an opportunity to witness the difference
between its doing and those having the same end in view, but
carried on without well-studied or sufficiently comprehensive
plans.

But in these Atlantic Floating Hospitals the difficulties were
very great. The desideratum is a practicable diet, simple yet
nourishing, abundant and not injurious; always ready, yet
varied enough to avoid the danger of satiety, which is ever
threatening the sick man, whose chance of recovery may hang
on his ability to eat his food with relish. In this arduous part
of the Hospital Transport duty, the ladies were able to be especially useful; their sympathy and good judgment coming constantly in play, and the supply of fruits, jellies, and a variety of
delicacies being generally so liberal as to afford full scope to
their powers. But in dealing with hundreds and thousands of
men, many of whom are not particularly in danger, but yet
obliged to lie in beds for wounds to heal, it is necessary to
provide on a scale so large as puts mere delicacies, or the ordinary resources of the sick room, quite out of the question. It is
utterly futile to attempt treating each one of four or five hundred patients as if we had him alone in a private family; and
patients, as well as nurse and friends, must learn this after
very little experience. But it is practicable here, as elsewhere,
to accomplish much that is beneficial and comfortable by judicious system firmly carried out. To avoid collisions, and vain
attempts to perform impossibilities, after a short experience,
but careful study of what was really needed, rules were established which proved in practice nearly perfect in the matter of
preventing delay and disappointment, while the result satisfied the patients in general quite as well as we can hope to satisfy sick men.

Olmstead, Frederick Law. *Hospital Transports*. Boston: Ticknor
    and Fields, 1863.

Specimen Days

by Walt Whitman

ARMY HOSPITALS LOOKED *for and accepted civilian volunteers to help in the care and comforting of the wounded and the sick. One of many that wandered the wards giving of time, money, and warmth was Walt Whitman—writer, philosopher, and poet. He was later to attain international fame for his writings. The best known of his works is* Leaves of Grass, *a book that he wrote and rewrote over a period of years.[1]*

Walt Whitman first moved to the hospital scene in 1862, when he helped nurse his wounded brother back to health. When the brother left for home to continue his convalescence, Whitman stayed on, roaming from hospital to hospital, helping in his own manner to bring comfort and encouragement to the sick troops. Some of the observations that follow were first printed in the newspaper The Brooklyn Daily Eagle *in New York City.*

---

[1] Whitman published *Leaves of Grass* himself in 1855. He published a longer edition in 1856 and continued to revise and add new poems until the final edition was published in 1892.

*Down at the Front, Falmouth, Va., opposite Fredericksburg,
December 21, 1862*

Begin my visits among the camp hospitals in the army of the
Potomac. Spend a good part of the day in a large brick
mansion on the banks of the Rappahannock, used as a hospital since the battle—seems to have receiv'd only the worst
cases. Out doors, at the foot of a tree within ten yards of the
front of the house, I notice a heap of amputated feet, legs,
arms, hands, &c., a full load for a one-horse cart. Several dead
bodies lie near, each cover'd with its brown woolen blanket.
In the door-yard, towards the river, are fresh graves, mostly of
officers, their names on pieces of barrel-staves or broken
boards, stuck in the dirt. (Most of these bodies were
subsequently taken up and transported north to their friends.)
The large mansion is quite crowded upstairs and down,
everything impromptu, no system, all bad enough, but I have
no doubt the best that can be done; all the wounds pretty bad,
some frightful, the men in their old clothes, unclean and
bloody. Some of the wounded are rebel soldiers and officers,
prisoners. One, a Mississippian, a captain, hit badly in leg, I
talk'd with some time; he ask'd me for papers, which I gave
him. (I saw him three months afterward in Washington, with
his leg amputated, doing well.) I went through the rooms,
downstairs and up. Some of the men were dying. I had
nothing to give at that visit, but wrote a few letters to folks,
home, mothers, &c. Also talk'd to three or four, who seem'd
most susceptible to it, and needing it.

After First Fredericksburg, December 23 to 31

The results of the late battle are exhibited everywhere about
here in thousands of cases, (hundreds die every day,) in the
camp, brigade, and division hospitals. These are merely tents,
and sometimes very poor ones, the wounded lying on the
ground, lucky if their blankets are spread on layers of pine or
hemlock twigs, or small leaves. No cots; seldom even a
mattress. It is pretty cold. The ground is frozen hard, and
there is occasional snow. I go around from one case to another.

I do not see that much good to these wounded and dying; but I cannot leave them. Once in a while some youngster holds on to me convulsively, and I do what I can for him; at any rate, stop with him and sit near him for hours, if he wishes it.

Besides the hospitals, I also go occasionally on long tours through the camps, talking with the men, &c. Sometimes at night among the groups around the fires, in their shebang enclosures of bushes, these are curious shows, full of characters and groups. I soon get acquainted anywhere in camp, with officers or men, and am always well used. Sometimes I go down on picket with the regiments I know best. As to rations, the army here at present seems to be tolerably well supplied, and the men have enough, such as it is, mainly salt pork and hard tack. Most of the regiments lodge in the flimsy little shelter tents. A few have built themselves huts of logs and mud with fire-places.

Back to Washington, January '63

Left camp at Falmouth, with some wounded, a few days since, and came here by Aquia creek railroad, and so on government steamer up the Potomac. Many wounded were with us on the cars and boat. The cars were just common platform ones. The railroad journey of ten or twelve miles was made mostly before sunrise. The soldiers guarding the road came out from their tents or shebangs of bushes with rumpled hair and half-awake look. Those on duty were walking their posts, some on banks over us, others down far below the level of the track. I saw large cavalry camps off the road. At Aquia creek landing were numbers of wounded going north. While I waited some three hours, I went around among them. Several wanted word sent home to parents, brothers, wives, &c., which I did for them, (by mail the next day from Washington.). On the boat I had my hands full. One poor fellow died going up.

I am now remaining in and around Washington, daily visiting the hospitals. Am much in Patent-office, Eighth Street, H Street, Armory-square, and others. Am now able to do a little good, having money, and getting experience. Today,

Sunday afternoon and till nine in the evening, visited Campbell
hospital; attended specially to one case in ward I, very sick
and pleurisy and typhoid fever, young man, farmer's son,
D. F. Russell, company E, 60th New York, downhearted and
feeble; a long time before he would take any interest; wrote a
letter home to his mother, in Malone, Franklin County, N. Y.,
at his request; gave him some fruit and one or two other gifts;
envelop'd and directed his letter, &c. Then went thoroughly
through ward 6, observ'd every case in the ward, without, I
think, missing one; gave perhaps from twenty to thirty persons,
each one some little gift, such as oranges, apples, sweet
crackers, figs, &c.

Thursday, Jan. 21

Devoted the main part of the day to Armory-square hospital; went pretty thoroughly through wards F, G, H, and I:
some fifty cases in each ward. In ward F supplied the men
throughout with writing paper and stamp'd envelope each;
distributed in small portions, to proper subjects, a large jar of
first-rate preserv'd berries, which had been donated to me by
a lady—her own cooking. Found several cases I thought good
subjects for small sums of money, which I furnish'd. (The
wounded men often come up broke, and it helps their spirits
to have even the small sum I give them.) My paper and
envelopes all gone, but distributed a good lot of amusing
reading matter; also, as I thought judicious, tobacco, oranges,
apples, &c. Interesting cases in ward I; Charles Miller, bed 19,
company D, 53d Pennsylvania, is only 16 years of age, very
bright, courageous boy, left leg amputated below the knee;
next bed to him, another young lad very sick; gave each
appropriate gifts. In the bed above, also, amputation of the left
leg; gave him a little jar of raspberries; bed 1, this ward, gave
small sum; also to a soldier on crutches, sitting on his bed
near . . . (I am more and more surprised at the very great proportion of youngsters from fifteen to twenty-one in the army. I
afterwards found a still greater proportion among the South-
erners.)

Evening, same day, went to see D. F. R., before alluded to; found him remarkable changed for the better; up and dress'd—quite a triumph; he afterwards got well, and went back to his regiment. Distributed in the wards a quantity of note-paper, and forty or fifty stamp'd envelopes, of which I had recruited my stock, and the men were much in need.

Fifty Hours Left Wounded on the Field

Here is the case of a soldier I found among the crowded cots in the Patent-office. He likes to have some one to talk to, and we will listen to him. He got badly hit in his leg and side at Fredericksburg that eventful Saturday, 13th of December. He lay the succeeding two days and nights helpless on the field, between the city and those grim terraces of batteries; his company and regiment had been compell'd to leave him to his fate. To make matters worse, it happen'd he lay with his head slightly down hill, and could not help himself. At the end of some fifty hours he was brought off, with other wounded under a flag of truce. I ask him how the rebels treated him as he lay during those two days and nights within reach of them—whether they came to him—whether they abused him? He answers that several of the rebels, soldiers and others, came to him at one time and another. A couple of them, who were together, spoke roughly and sarcastically but nothing worse. One middle aged man, however, who seem'd to be moving around the field, among the dead and wounded, for benevolent purposes, came to him in a way he will never forget; treated our soldier kindly, bound up his wounds, cheer'd him, gave him a couple of biscuits and a drink of whiskey and water; asked him if he could eat some beef. This good secesh, however, did not change our soldier's position, for it might have caused the blood to burst from the wounds, clotted and stagnated. Our soldier is from Pennsylvania; has had a pretty severe time; the wounds proved to be bad ones. But he retains a good heart, and is at present on the gain. (It is not uncommon for the men to remain on the field this way, one, two, or even four or five days.)

Hospital Scenes and Persons, Wednesday, February 4th

Visited Armory-square hospital, went pretty thoroughly
through wards E and D. Supplied paper and envelopes to all
who wish'd—as usual, found plenty of men who needed
those articles. Wrote letters. Saw and talk'd with two or three
members of the Brooklyn 14th regt. A poor fellow in ward D,
with a fearful wound in a fearful condition, was having some
loose splinters of bone taken from the neighborhood of the
wound. The operation was long, and one of great pain—yet,
after it was well commenced, the soldier bore it in silence. He
sat up, propp'd—was much wasted—had lain a long time
quiet in one position (not for days only but weeks,) a blood-
less, brown-skinn'd face, with eyes full of determination—
belong'd to a New York regiment. There was an unusual
cluster of surgeons, medical cadets, nurses, &c., around his
bed—I thought the whole thing was done with tenderness,
and done well. In one case, the wife sat by the side of her hus-
band, his sickness typhoid fever, pretty bad. In another, by the
side of her son, a mother—she told me she had seven children, and this was the youngest. (A fine, kind, healthy, gentle
mother, good-looking, not very old, with a cap on her head,
and dress'd like home—what a charm it gave to the whole
ward.) I liked the woman nurse in ward E —I noticed how she
sat a long time by a poor fellow who just had, that morning,
in addition to his other sickness, bad hemorrhage—she gently
assisted him, reliev'd him of the blood, holding a cloth
to his mouth, as he coughed it up—he was so weak he could
only just turn his head over on the pillow.

One young New York man with a bright, handsome face,
had been lying several months from a most disagreeable
wound, receiv'd at Bull Run. A bullet had shot him right
through the bladder, hitting him front, low in the belly, and
coming out back. He had suffer'd much—the water came out
of the wound, by slow but steady quantities, for many
weeks—so that he lay almost constantly in a sort of puddle—
and there were other disagreeable circumstances. He was of

good heart, however. At present comparatively comfortable, had a bad throat, was delighted with a stick of horehound candy I gave him, with one or two other trifles.

A Night Battle, Over a Week Since, May 12, '63

There was part of the late battle at Chancellorsville, (second Fredericksburg,) a little over a week ago, Saturday, Saturday night and Sunday, under Gen. Joe Hooker, I would like to give just a glimpse of—(a moment's look in a terrible storm at sea—of which a few suggestions are enough, and full details impossible.) The fighting had been very hot during the day, and after an intermission the later part, was resumed at night, and kept up with furious energy till 3 o'clock in the morning. That afternoon (Saturday) an attack sudden and strong by Stonewall Jackson had gain'd a great advantage to the Southern army, and broken our lines, entering us like a wedge, and leaving things in that position at dark. But Hooker at 11 at night made a desperate push, drove the secesh forces back, restored his original lines, and resumed his plans. This night scrimmage was very exciting, and afforded countless strange and fearful pictures. The fighting had been general both at Chancellorsville and northeast at Fredericksburg. (We hear of some poor fighting, episodes, skedaddling on our part. I think not of it. I think of the fierce bravery, the general rule.) One corps, the 6th, Sedgewick's, fights four dashing and bloody battles in thirty-six hours, retreating in great jeopardy, losing largely but maintaining itself, fighting with the sternest desperation under all circumstances, getting over the Rappahannock only by the skin of its teeth, yet getting over. It lost many, many brave men, yet it took vengeance, ample vengeance.

But it was the tug of Saturday evening, and through the night and Sunday morning, I wanted to make a special note of. It was largely in the woods, and quite a general engagement. The night was very pleasant, at times the moon shining

out full and clear, all Nature so calm in itself, the early summer grass so rich, and foliage of the trees—yet there the battle
raging, and many good fellows lying helpless, with new
accessions to them, and every minute, amid the rattle of mus-
kets and crash of cannon, (for there was an artillery contest
too,) the red life-blood oozing out from heads or trunks or
limbs upon that green and dew-cool grass. Patches of the
woods take fire, and several of the wounded, unable to move,
are consumed—quite large spaces are swept over, burning the
dead also—some of the men have their hair and beards
singed—some, burns on their faces and hands—others holes
burnt in their clothing. The flashes of fire from the cannon, the
quick flaring flames and smoke, and the immense roar—the
musketry so general, the light nearly bright enough for each
side to see the other—the crashing, tramping of men—the
yelling—close quarters—we hear the secesh yells—our men
cheer loudly back, especially if Hooker is in sight—hand to
hand conflicts, each side stands up to it, brave, determin'd as
demons, they often charge upon us—a thousand deeds
are done worth to write newer greater poems on—and still the
woods on fire—still many are not only scorch'd—too many,
unable to move, are burned to death.

Then the camps of the wounded—O heavens, what scene is
this?—is this indeed *humanity*—these butcher's shambles?
There are several of them. There they lie, in the largest, in an
open space in the woods, from 200 to 300 poor fellows—the
groans and screams—the odor of blood, mixed with the fresh
scent of the night, the grass, the trees—that slaughter-house!
O well is it their mothers, their sisters cannot see them—cannot conceive, and never conceiv'd, these things. One man is
shot by a shell, both in the arm and leg—both are amputated—there lie the rejected members. Some have their legs
blown off—some bullets through the breast—some indescrib-
ably horrid wounds in the face or head, all mutilated, sicken-
ing, torn, gouged out—some in the abdomen—some mere
boys—many rebels, badly hurt—they take their regular turns
with the rest, just the same as any—the surgeons use them just
the same. Such is the camp of the wounded—such a fragment,

a reflection afar off of the bloody scene—while all over the
clear, large moon comes out at times softly, quietly shining.
Amid the woods, that scene of flitting souls—amid the crack
and crash and yelling sounds—the impalpable perfume of the
woods—and yet the pungent, stifling smoke—the radiance of
the moon, looking from heaven at intervals so placid—the sky
so heavenly—the clear-obscure up there, those buoyant upper
oceans—a few large placid stars beyond, coming silently and
languidly out, and then disappearing—the melancholy,
draperied night above, around. And there, upon the roads, the
fields, and in those woods, that contest, never one more desperate in any age or land—both parties now in force—
masses—no fancy battle, no semiplay, but fierce and savage
demons fighting there—courage and scorn of death the rule,
exceptions almost none.

What history, I say, can ever give—for who can know—the
mad, determin'd tussle of the armies, in all their separate
large and little squads—as this—each steep'd from crown to
toe in desperate, mortal purports? Who know the conflict,
hand to hand—the many conflicts in the dark, those shadowy-
tangled, flashing moonbeam'd woods—the writhing groups
and squads—the cries, the din, the cracking guns and pis-
tols—the distant cannon—the cheers and calls and threats and
awful music of the oaths—the indescribable mix—the officers'
orders, persuasions, encouragements—the devils fully rous'd
in human hearts—the strong shout, *Charge, men, charge*—the
flash of the naked sword, and rolling flame and smoke? And
still the broken, clear and clouded heaven—and still again the
moonlight pouring silvery soft its radiant patches over all.
Who paint the scene, the sudden partial panic of the afternoon, at dusk? Who paint the irrepressible advance of the second division of the Third corps, under Hooker himself,
suddenly order'd up—those rapid-filing phantoms through
the woods? Who show what moves there in the shadows,
fluid and firm—to save, (and it did save,) the army's name,
perhaps the nation? as there the veterans hold the field.
(Brave Berry falls not yet—but death has mark'd him—soon
he falls.)

Unnamed Remains the Bravest Soldier

Of scenes like these, I say, who writes—whoe'er can write
the story? Of many a score—aye, thousands, North and South,
of unwrit heroes, unknown heroisms, incredible, impromptu,
first-class desperations—who tells? No history ever—no poem
sings, no music sounds, those bravest men of all—those
deeds. No formal general's report, nor book in the library, nor
column in the paper, embalms the bravest, North or South,
East or West. Unnamed, unknown, remain and still remain,
the bravest soldiers. Our manliest—our boys—our hardy dar-
lings; no picture gives them. Likely, the typic one of them
(standing, no doubt, for hundreds, thousands,) crawls aside to
some bush-clump, or ferny tuft, on receiving his death-shot—
there sheltering a little while, soaking roots, grass, and soil,
with red blood—the battle advances, retreats, flits from the
scene, sweeps by—and there, haply with pain and suffering
(yet less, far less, than is supposed,) the last lethargy winds
like a serpent round him—the eyes glaze in death—none
recks—perhaps the burial-squads, in truce, a week afterwards,
search not the secluded spot—and there, at last, the Bravest
Soldier crumbles in mother earth, unburied and unknown.

A Sight in Camp in the Daybreak Gray and Dim

A sight in camp in the daybreak gray and dim,
As from my tent I emerge so early sleepless,
As slow I walk in the cool fresh air the path near by the
      hospital tent,
Three forms I see on stretchers lying, brought out there
      untended lying,
Over each the blanket spread, ample brownish woolen blanket,
Gray and heavy blanket, folding, covering all.

Curious I halt and silent stand,
Then with light fingers I from the face of the nearest the first
      just lift the blanket;

Who are you elderly man so gaunt and grim, with well-gray'd hair,
    and flesh all sunken about the eyes?
Who are you my dear comrade?
Then to the second I step—and who are you my child and darling?
Who are you sweet boy with cheeks yet blooming?
Then to the third—a face nor child nor old, very calm, as of
    beautiful yellow-white ivory;
Young man I think I know you—I think this face is the face
    of the Christ himself.
Dead and divine and brother of all, and here again he lies.

                          —*Walt Whitman, 1865*

Whitman, Walt. *Specimen Days: The Complete Prose Works of Walt Whitman*, Vol. 1. New York: G. P. Putnam's Sons, 1902.

Bibliography

Adams, George Worthington. *Doctors in Blue.* New York: Henry Schuman, Inc., 1952.

Bigelow, John. *France and the Confederate Navy: 1862–1868 An International Episode.* New York: Harper and Brothers, 1888.

Billings, John D. *Hardtack and Coffee.* Bloomington, Ind.: Indiana University Press, 1961.

Blay, John S. *The Civil War.* New York: Bonanza Books, 1958.

Boyer, Samuel Pellman. *Naval Surgeon: Blockading the South: 1862–1866.* Edited by Elinor Barnes and James A. Barnes. Bloomington, Ind.: Indiana University Press, 1963.

Bridgewater, William, and Elizabeth J. Sherwood, eds. *The Columbia Encyclopedia.* New York: Columbia University Press, 1950.

Brinton, John H. *Personal Memoirs of John H. Brinton.* New York: The Neale Publishing Co., 1914.

Brockett, L. P. and Mary C. Vaughan: Introduction by Henry W. Bellows, D.D. *Woman's Work in the Civil War: A Record of Heroism, Patriotism and Patience.* Philadelphia: Zeigler, McCurdy and Company, 1867.

Brockett, Linus Pierpont. *The Camp, the Battle-Field and the Hospital.*

Brooks, Stewart. *Civil War Medicine.* Springfield, Ill.: Charles C. Thomas, Publisher, 1966.

Butterfield, Roger. *The American Past.* New York: Simon and Schuster, 1957.

Catton, Bruce. *Terrible Swift Sword,* vol. 2. New York: Doubleday and Company, Inc., 1963.

Catton, Bruce. *The American Heritage Picture History of the Civil War,* vols. 1 and 2. Edited by Richard M. Ketchum. New York: American Heritage Publishing Co., 1960.

Cunningham, H. H. *Doctors in Gray.* Baton Rouge: Louisiana State University Press, 1958.

Davis, William C. *Fighting Men of the Civil War.* London: Salamander Books, 1989.

Edmonds, S. Emma E. *Nurse and Spy in the Union Army: Comprising the Adventures and Experiences of a Woman in Hospitals, Camps, and Battle-Fields.* Hartford, Conn.: W. S. Williams and Company, 1865.

Fox, William F. *Final Report on the Battlefield of Gettysburg; New York Monument Commission for the Battlefields of Gettysburg and Chattanooga,* vols. 1 and 2. Albany, N.Y.: J. B. Lyon Company, 1902.

Hamilton, Frank Hastings, M.D. *A Treatise on Military Surgery and Hygiene.* New York: Bailliere Brothers, 1865.

Livermore, Mary A. *My Story of the War: A Woman's Narrative of Four Years Personal Experience.* Hartford, Conn.: A. D. Worthington and Company, 1889.

Locke, E. W. *Three Years in Camp and Hospital.* Boston: Geo. D. Russell and Co., 1870.

Long, E. B. *The Civil War Day by Day: An Almanac 1861–1865.* New York: Da Capo, 1985.

Moore, Frank. *The Civil War in Song and Story. 1860–1865.* New York: P. F. Collier, 1889.

One Hundred Years of American Independence. New York: A. S. Barnes and Company, 1876.

Ropes, Hannah. *Civil War Nurse: The Diary and Letters of Hannah Ropes.* Edited by John R. Brumgardt. Knoxville, Tenn.: University of Tennessee Press, 1980.

Sandburg, Carl. *Abraham Lincoln: The Prairie Years and the War Years.* New York: Harcourt, Brace and World, Inc., 1954.

Steiner, Paul. *Diseases in the Civil War.* Springfield, Ill. Charles C. Thomas, Publisher, 1968.

Straubing, Harold Elk. *Civil War Eyewitness Reports.* Hamden, Conn.: Archon Books, 1985.

Westrate, E. V. *Those Fatal Generals.* New York: Knight Publications, 1936.

Wiley, Bell Irvin. *The Common Soldier in the Civil War.* New York: Bobbs Merrill Company, Inc., 1943.

Index